Dr Peter Vardy is Vice Principal of Heythrop College, University of London. He lectures in Philosophy of Religion and is the Course Director for the University's External Theology Programme as well as a former Chair of the Board of Theological Studies of the University.

'Dr Peter Vardy is a modern-day Socrates. *The Puzzle of God* presents complex theological issues in a manner which is both exciting and relevant. It is an invaluable resource for any serious student of philosophy of religion. Demanding philosophical issues are clearly presented in an accessible way without sacrificing detailed analysis ... as a popularizer of philosophy of religion Peter Vardy is unsurpassed.'

John Waters, joint editor of *Dialogue* magazine

'This is a masterpiece of coherence. Step by step the reader is led clearly and humorously through the philosophical maze which confuses our thinking about God ... an invaluable resource.'

Linda Smith, Kings College, London

'This is about the best elementary textbook on the philosophy of God I have come across. It shows a special flair for reducing apparently complex arguments to their simplest elements ... an extremely useful book.'

Professor Hugo Meynell

'A lucid and challenging exposition.'

John McDade, editor of *The Month*

'An accomplished guide around the battlefield of ideas about God.'

Don Cupitt

The Puzzle of God

PETER VARDY

Fount

An Imprint of HarperCollins*Publishers*

Fount Paperbacks is an Imprint of
HarperCollins*Religious*
Part of HarperCollins*Publishers*
77–85 Fulham Palace Road, London W6 8JB

First published in Great Britain in 1990 by Flame,
expanded and revised edition published in 1995
by Fount

This revised edition 1999

7 9 10 8 6

© 1990, 1995, 1999 Peter Vardy

Peter Vardy asserts the moral right to be
identified as the author of this work

A catalogue record for this book is
available from the British Library

ISBN 0 00 628143 5

Printed and bound in Great Britain by
Clays Ltd, St Ives plc

Contents

LETTER TO THE READER

Dear Reader,

Throughout the centuries poets, playwrights, prophets, writers and saints have sought to communicate the reality of God to the world. Today we live in a rational age and their voices are muted. Still the eternal questions remain to challenge us and to mock the shortness of our brief lives.

This book tries to present, clearly and simply, the main features of many of the central debates concerning God's reality and how God is to be understood. No answers are given – rather the aim is to help you, the reader, to think through the problems for yourself. Wherever specialised terms are used, they are defined so that no previous knowledge or reading is required.

The search for truth is never a comfortable one. It is always easier and more secure not to think and to remain content with our own certainties. Yet, whether we are believers or non-believers, doubts and problems about our own positions creep into our minds, however much we may try to avoid thinking about them. If there is a creator God, surely God has created our minds, and so any search for truth should not lead us away from God. If there is no creator God, we have only ourselves on whom to depend. The search for truth and meaning is one of the few things that endure in a transitory world. As the book of Proverbs says when talking about wisdom:

Receive my instruction and not silver;
and knowledge rather than choice gold.
For wisdom is better than rubies;
and all the things that may be desired are not to be compared to it
(Proverbs 8:10–11).

This book is a small attempt to help in the search for understanding. It is a search that will never be completely achieved, but this does not mean that the attempt must not be made. I hope you find the quest as exciting and worthwhile as I do.

This book was first published in 1990, revised in 1995 with a new postscript and substantially rewritten in 1999. Through these years I have lectured at Heythrop College, part of the University of London, which specialises in philosophy and theology. I owe an enormous debt to Heythrop and to all the friends I have made there, as well as to others, for their advice and the discussions we have shared over the years.

Peter Vardy
Heythrop College, University of London
Pentecost 1999

SECTION 1

PHILOSOPHIC
BACKGROUND

ONE
Unicorns, Numbers and God

1 a) I believe in God.
   b) I do not believe in God.

2 a) I believe in unicorns.
   b) I do not believe in unicorns.

We all know what a unicorn is. If we met one walking down our local High Street we would recognise it. We might, of course, have some doubts as to whether it was a real unicorn. We might well suspect that it was a trick of some sort, and might imagine that what we saw was a horse with a spiral horn somehow grafted onto its forehead. However, there would be tests that we could apply, and these might well include finding out where the animal came from. It may well be that we think that meeting a unicorn is so unlikely that no tests would satisfy us. In this case we would be sceptical about the possibility of unicorns. We would agree about what a unicorn would be like, but we would simply deny that there were such animals!

Imagine that you have a friend who is useless at mathematics. As soon as he sees a mathematical symbol, his mind goes blank. He has no notion of the basic elements of mathematics, although he is otherwise intelligent. Imagine that you try to explain to him what a prime number is. You might say: 'A prime number is any whole number that is divisible by itself and one and by no other number.' You might go on to give examples and to tell him that the numbers 2, 3, 5, 7, 11, 13, 17, 19 and so on are prime numbers. The person to

3

whom you are explaining might, however, not be able to make anything of all this talk – to him, prime numbers are simply not real. They are a curious idea used by mathematicians – they are simply irrelevant and make no sense to him. Finally, he might say to you: 'You say prime numbers are real and that they exist. All right, show me one.' You will probably be puzzled by this. You can't put him in a car and drive him to see the prime number 23. Prime numbers certainly exist, but you cannot go to visit them. The prime number 23, or any other prime number, is not sitting in a particular place. The very fact that he asks you to show him a prime number means that he has not understood what a prime number is.

We understand what unicorns are and most of us accept that they do not exist. We understand what prime numbers are and most of us accept that prime numbers exist – albeit in a different way to unicorns. We understand that trees, love, atoms and evil exist – but in different ways. What, however, does it mean to talk of God existing?

The word 'God' has been the most fought-over and debated word in the history of ideas. For centuries it dominated the thought of the most intelligent people on this planet. Even today, talk about God is guaranteed to raise the passions. Religion is an emotive subject, and around the world families and communities are divided from each other because of different religious beliefs. All too often these beliefs are passionately held, yet all too rarely do those holding the beliefs stop to think about what it is that they believe.

Even within a particular community people will differ about what the word 'God' means. Many people have a somewhat childish idea of God, seeing Him as an old man with a white beard sitting somewhere above the clouds. If we talk to someone else about God, we will normally find considerable differences between the two of us, and examining these differences with an open mind can help each of us to be clear about what we do and do not believe.

Philosophy is partly concerned with a search for truth and under-standing. This book takes the search seriously. There is no hidden agenda, no attempt to provide you with the 'right' answer. Rather, the aim is to help you, the reader, to think through what God means and then to go on to explore the consequences of holding this view. Whatever view you hold is going to be fraught with difficulties and complications. Some people are nervous of philosophy because they do not think it is right to think about or to examine their faith. However, most religions make a claim to truth, and so this claim should be taken seriously. Any religion that seeks truth should not be frightened of the search for greater understanding. Samuel Taylor Coleridge put it this way: 'He who begins by loving Christianity better than truth will proceed by loving his own sect or Church better than Christianity and end by loving himself better than all.'

If we refuse to seek the truth, if we retreat behind our own certainties because we are frightened that they cannot bear examination, then we are likely to become increasingly intolerant of others. In a world where there are many different religious systems, the search for truth and understanding must be a worthy one. In previous centuries, religious wars were used by one religious grouping to impose their beliefs on others. Human beings should have moved beyond that stage now, although, sadly, this is not the case. We should be able to sit down with friends who have different religious beliefs and reason our way towards greater mutual understanding.

The chapters that follow look at three different ideas of what it means to talk about God. All these ideas are persuasive, all are influential. Some have an ancient history, others have their roots in the past but have been more recently brought up to date. All are credible, all suffer from disadvantages. In exploring these different ideas of God we will be exploring the very heart of religion and, by so doing, we may be able to come closer to the goal of our own search for ultimate truth.

Questions for consideration

a) What does it mean to say that God exists? Is God more like a spirit, a person, a prime number, an idea in people's minds or none of these?

b) If religious believers hold fast to certain beliefs, does it matter if these are true?

c) Can it ever be right to believe in a particular way of looking at the world and not to think about one's beliefs or not to listen to the points of view of others?

d) Are the beliefs of our parents and those beliefs with which we have been brought up necessarily right?

TWO

What is Truth?

One way of learning to swim is to be thrown into the deep end! We are going straight into a discussion which is probably going to be at the heart of philosophy and theology in the next century, yet few people are aware of the issues. It really revolves around the question Pontius Pilate asked Jesus during his trial: 'What is truth?' (cf. my book *What is truth?*, University of New South Wales, 1999). This is tremendously important, particularly when we start to consider what it means to say that a religious or a moral claim is true.

To understand the issues, we are going to have to think about how language is used. We learn language at our parents' knees. Very young children have an innate ability to master language. This mastery is one of the key elements in human development. Early man developed an ability to wield tools, but as the first inarticulate grunts developed into a means of communication, so it became possible for individuals to co-operate towards some common end. Language is a public affair. It is the way in which we communicate ideas, aspirations, truths, objectives and insights. We use language to tell others of our needs, feelings and intentions.

Language is not static, it is developing all the time. New words are introduced and the meanings of old words change. The meaning of the term a 'gay young man' a hundred years ago was entirely different to what it is today. Even 30 years ago, a billion in Britain meant a million million. Today Britain has adopted the United States convention and a billion means a thousand million – a substantial difference. Terms like 'genetic engineering', 'embryo research', 'laptop computer', 'mobile telephone', 'charged particles', 'acid rain' or 'video recorder' simply did not exist until recently, as the ideas they represented were not there to be expressed. Language is rich and it is dynamic. It expresses truth and also, of course, falsity. However, what does it mean for language to express truth? Take a simple statement like 'Murder is wrong.' What does it mean to say that this statement is true? Most people would probably agree with this claim, but that does not mean that we understand what would be necessary to make the statement true.

There are two basic theories of truth, or ways of understanding truth:

The correspondence theory of truth

The correspondence theory of truth maintains that a statement is true if it corresponds to a state of affairs which it attempts to describe. Thus 'The dog sits on the bench' is true iff (this means 'if and only if') what I am referring to is a dog and it is sitting on the bench. Truth does not depend on language and the society in which we live. Someone who holds to a correspondence theory of truth is today called a *realist*.

Realists maintain that language captures reality, it does not create reality. Language attempts to stretch out to a reality that is external to us and tries to express this reality accurately. Sometime we make errors – for instance, people once believed that the world was flat. This view was mistaken, those who hold to the correspondence theory will maintain, because the world is *not* flat. The error lay in people thinking that the claim to flatness correctly represented the world, when it did not.

The realist will maintain that a statement is *either* true *or* false. This is to affirm *bivalence*. Bivalence means that the truth or falsity of a statement does not depend on evidence. Evidence will help us to decide whether a statement is true or not, but truth does not depend on evidence. Take the statements 'Caesar ate an apple on the morning he landed in Britain' or 'There is intelligent life elsewhere in the universe.' Realists maintain that these statements are either true or they are false. Certainly there may be no evidence of their truth or falsity, but this does not maintain there is not a truth at stake.

To talk of truth is to claim that language correctly corresponds to the reality that lies beyond it. On this basis, the statement 'I am sitting on a chair' is true if and only if what I am sitting on is a chair. This seems obvious, but it need not be. In some societies, they may have no idea of chairs, they may never sit down. We could easily imagine the society of ancient Rome where everyone lay down to have meals and the alternatives were between standing and lying down. If someone from such a society were shown a chair she would not know what it was, and might instead regard it as a thing which one stands on in order to make oneself higher, in other words a form of pedestal. Truth, it might be claimed, is expressed in language and language is used in different ways in different societies. It is this claim that leads on to the alternative conception of truth.

The coherence theory of truth

The coherence theory of truth maintains that a statement is true if it coheres with other true statements. Someone who holds a coherence theory of truth is today called an *anti-realist*. Imagine a jigsaw. One piece of a jigsaw belongs or is correct only if it fits in with other pieces. Jigsaw pieces are not isolated, they are part of a dynamic whole. All the definitions in a dictionary are in fact circular, since they are all expressed in words, and each of those words is defined by other words. There is no word that cannot be defined using other words.

The coherence theory of truth says that the same sort of principle applies to language. Language is the jigsaw into which words and expressions have to fit. A word that does not fit in does not make any sense. The statement about the world being flat, the anti-realist claims, would once have been true because it formed an integral part of the way in which the world was then seen. It was once true, but is so no longer.

According to this theory a statement is true if it coheres or fits in with other statements considered to be true within a particular form of life. Take the case of morality. If you are a Roman Catholic, then the statement 'artificial birth control is wrong' will be true for you. (You may not, of course, choose to obey this moral rule, but it is nevertheless a rule which forms part of the Catholic way of life.) Similarly, it is true that you have a duty to go to Mass on Sunday and on Holy Days of obligation. If you are a Hindu, it is true that you must respect cows. If you are a Muslim, then it is true that you have an obligation to pray facing towards Mecca and, and so far as this is possible, to make a pilgrimage to Mecca at least once during your lifetime. For a Muslim it is true that a man may have four wives but for a Christian it is true that only one is allowed.

What makes these statements true is that they are part of or fit in with a particular form of life. Within the Catholic, Hindu or Islamic worlds, within their different forms of life, these statements are true. On this basis, there can be different truths in different communities. Truth is not absolute, it is relative. Truth in one culture may be different from truth in another.

Take the example of two posts with another post joining them across the top. In a society where football is played, this might be considered a goalpost. What makes this arrangement a goalpost is how the society uses the term, and the use it has for the idea of goal-posts. In a society which does not play football, the same arrangement might be correctly termed 'washing-line'. In another society it might be called 'execution place' – because it is the place from which people are hung by ropes suspended from the crossbar. Whether it is goalpost, washing-line or execution place depends on the society in which it is used.

The anti-realists hold that truth is relative to the form of life or the community in which the truth claims are made or expressed. Within a particular form of life, within a particular society, something may be true which is not true elsewhere. Anti-realists deny bivalence (this was defined earlier in this chapter), since they claim that some statements are neither true nor false – they just have no content. It is neither true nor false for a tribe of Amazonian Indians who have never seen an outsider before, that the three poles referred to above are a goal. The idea of goalposts has simply no meaning for them, and the question of truth or falsity does not, therefore, arise.

If we consider the moral arena, the issue may be clearer. Take the following statements:

1 Sex before marriage is wrong.
2 Homosexuality is wrong.
3 Killing your parents is wrong.

The realist will maintain that these statements are either true or false and that their truth or falsity does not depend on the society in which they are expressed. Beyond any of our earthly societies, they might perhaps claim, there is a transcendental realm of value which makes moral statements either true or false. If they do not correspond, they are false. The realist will claim that the moral values of different societies are right or wrong to the extent that they correspond to some ultimate value. This ultimate value may be found

* in the will of God who has laid down absolute moral rules, or
* in something like Plato's Forms which exist beyond time and space and which represent the perfect ideas of truth, justice, the good, etc., and to which our moral claims need to conform if they are to be true.

The anti-realist will reply, 'Oh no, this is not the case at all. Within some societies sex before marriage, homosexuality and killing your parents is wrong, but in other societies these may be right. There are no absolutes. There is no independent standard or vantage point from which or by which we can judge moral norms. Morality evolves to meet the needs of society and in different societies there may be different moralities. A hundred years ago sex before marriage was wrong. Today, in the Western world, it is morally acceptable between two people who love each other and who are in a long-term relationship. In some African societies, sex before marriage is the accepted norm.'

If there are disagreements about morality between different societies, the realist will claim that one society is right and the others are wrong, as there can be only one truth. The anti-realist will say that there is no single truth – within each society there are true and valid positions, and you cannot judge the morality of one society by the ideas of another.

Truth about the future

Someone can be a realist about some things and an anti-realist about others. For instance, someone can be a realist about morality but an anti-realist about the future. Take the statement 'Judith will have 14 children' made about a girl who is presently aged 19 and who is biologically capable of having children if the circumstances are right:

1 The realist about the future will maintain that it is either true or false *now* that Judith will have 14 children, even if we do not know which is the case. Somehow, the realist will maintain, there exists a fact 'out there' to which the statement 'Judith will have 14 children' corresponds. We may not have the evidence to tell whether or not this statement is true, but lack of evidence does not prevent the realist saying that the statement is either true or false.

2 The anti-realist will simply deny that there is any truth to be known, since there is no fact 'out there' and there is no evidence that could count for or against the statement about the number of children that Judith will eventually have. The statement is neither true nor false.

Making sense of mistakes

The issue of how the realist and the anti-realist make sense of mistakes is important. Both realist and anti-realist recognise that mistakes can be made, but their understanding is different:

1 The realist will seek to justify the truth of a statement by establishing its correspondence with the independent reality to which it is held to relate. A statement will be false if it fails to correspond to the reality that lies beyond language. Even when the realist has exhausted *all* available verification conditions, she will still say, 'But I could still be wrong.' Truth, for the realist, transcends (or goes beyond) the verification conditions that are or could be available and a *global mistake* is always possible. A global mistake is a total mistake, a mistake made even after every available or possible checking procedure has been correctly carried out.

2 The anti-realist will seek to establish the truth of a statement by determining whether it coheres or fits in with other true statements – whether, in other words, it fits in with the jigsaw which is the form of life of the particular society.

For the anti-realist, a statement is false if it fails to cohere with other true statements within a particular society. The anti-realist checks whether the statement does correctly cohere by applying verification procedures to test the statement against other statements accepted as true within the society concerned.

Once the anti-realist has exhausted all the possible or available checks (the conditions or tests that would verify whether the statement fits into the jigsaw), then the statement is simply held to be true. To continue to say, 'Well, we have exhausted the checks – we have used every means to ensure that the statement does cohere with other true statements – but are we *sure* it is true?' simply does not make sense, since truth *is* coherence with other true statements in a particular society or form of life.

A global mistake is, for the anti-realist, impossible. Once we are certain, by applying all the available or possible checking procedures (there is a difference to explore here), that the statement does cohere with other true statements, then the statement in question is simply true.

The difference between realist and anti-realist can be illustrated by the belief in a flat earth which we have used as an example. If we had lived a thousand years ago, all the tests that would have been available would have served to demonstrate that the world was flat. Everyone would have agreed and the evidence would have been overwhelming. The anti-realist would have maintained that in the society in which people were then living it was true to say that the world was flat. The realist, whilst accepting that all the available evidence pointed in this direction, would still have said, 'But I could still be wrong.' The eventual discovery that the earth was in fact round would, for the realist, have shown that the original claim that the earth was flat was an error, a mistake. It was not correct because the statement did not correspond to the state of the world.

Summary

There are two different ways of looking at what it means to say that a statement is true:

1 The realist claims that a statement is true because it corresponds to a state of affairs that is independent of language and of the society in which we live. To say that a statement is true is to claim that it correctly refers beyond itself.

2 The anti-realist claims that a statement is true because it coheres with other true statements within a particular society or form of life. To say that a statement is true is to claim that it fits in or coheres with other statements.

When we come to apply this to God, we shall see that the realist maintains that the statement 'God exists' is true because it corresponds or refers to the God who created and sustains the universe. The anti-realist, on the other hand, will claim that 'God exists' is true because the statement coheres or fits in with other statements made by religious believers. As we shall see, the two positions are very different!

Questions for consideration

a) What would one do to establish whether it is true to say 'Thou shalt not steal?' Do you think the truth of this statement depends on the society in which one lives?

b) Are you a realist or an anti-realist about the future? Why?

c) What is bivalence?

d) If all the possible checks have been carried out to ensure that a statement is true, is it still possible that the statement could nevertheless be false? Give examples.

THREE

The Background to
the Debate about God

If you ask someone who speaks Chinese to write down the Chinese symbol for God, he or she may well say, 'Which one? The Catholic or the Protestant God?' The Chinese language has a character for each of the two different Gods. Many Christians, of course, would say that this is a mistake and that both Protestant and Catholics worship the same God. This, however, is oversimplistic. There is an enormous difference between the God of traditional Catholic theology and the God with which many Protestants identify, although many Catholics worship the Protestant idea of God and many Protestants think in terms of the Catholic view. The next three chapters will examine three different conceptions of what it means to talk of God. In a way this book is unusual as it is possibly the only book dealing with the philosophy of religion that maintains that it is essential to work out what 'God' means before tackling any other problems in the philosophy of religion. Many books on philosophy and theology use the word 'God', but few spell out what this word means. Where content is given to the word, usually only one understanding will be given. The aim of the next three chapters is to help you explore the alternatives because, as will become clear, this will be vital in discussing every other issue in the philosophy of religion. Before doing this, however, it is important to lay some historical foundations. It has been said by the British philosopher Whitehead that all Western philosophy is really a series of footnotes to Plato and Aristotle. We need to start by looking at their two different positions.

Plato

Plato was born in 427 BCE (this means 'Before the Christian Era' and is written like this instead of the previously used BC which means 'Before Christ' as this was considered to give offence to those of other faiths) and died in 347 BCE. He was a native of Athens and came from a noble family. He became a pupil of Socrates. After Socrates was condemned to death for, among other things, 'corrupting the young', by getting them to think for themselves and to challenge the views of their parents and elders (the aim of a good philosophy of religion teacher may well be to 'corrupt the young' by helping young people to think for themselves, to probe and question the values and beliefs of their parents and the society in which they live; this can be an uncomfortable business and it is not surprising that Socrates was sentenced to death), Plato withdrew from Athens and travelled for a number of years. Eventually he returned to his native city and established a school on the outskirts near the grove sacred to Academus. This school, 'The Academy', remained in existence until it was dissolved by the Roman Emperor Justinian in 529.

Plato's god was called the Demiurge. The Demiurge did not create matter. Raw matter had always existed in a state of chaos. The Demiurge took this matter and moulded it rather like a potter moulds clay. The potter does not make the clay, but he makes things with it. So the Demiurge used pre-existing matter to fashion the universe. He also enabled the universe to share in his perfection by putting into it mind or soul, which would not otherwise be present in raw matter.

The Demiurge had a model to work from. Plato considered that matter, being in time and space, imperfectly resembled the perfect heavenly Forms which existed outside time and space. Time was 'the moving image of eternity' – but it was only an image of the eternal Forms, and could not be identical with them. People saw, in the universe, examples of the perfect, timeless and spaceless Forms of Truth, Justice, Beauty and the Good (notice that the Forms are written with a capital letter – thus something that was beautiful here on earth imperfectly resembled or participated in the Form of Beauty). The Forms were not created by the Demiurge and they did not 'do' anything. The Forms did not create, nor were they created, they were simply there. The Demiurge used them as a model after which to fashion or make the universe. However, he had a problem.

The Forms were *timeless* (outside time, so that time did not pass for them), *spaceless* (outside space, you could not, therefore, visit one of the Platonic Forms, however far you travelled in a spaceship) and *immutable* (unchanging in every respect). The material that the Demiurge had to work with, on the other hand, was temporal and spatial. So the Demiurge had to use imperfect materials to fashion something to resemble the perfect, unchanging original. The universe necessarily, therefore, had to be an imperfect model, because it was in time and space whilst the Forms were not. It is as if a sculptor were asked to make a bronze statue of the wind. Somehow he has to capture in brass the expression of something which is ephemeral, fleeting and changing all the time. He might, for instance, produce a statue of a young girl with her long hair being blown free behind her, or one of a tree bending in the wind. The finished sculpture might well capture something of the flavour and power of the wind, but it could not be an altogether accurate picture. Similarly, the Demiurge had to capture in a moving and changing temporal material the essence of something totally unchanging.

The Demiurge did as good a job as he could, but inevitably, given the material he was working with, it was not perfect. This, Plato thought, accounted for many of the imperfections in the world.

The instances of beauty, truth, justice, goodness and similar qualities with which we are familiar on earth are obviously not perfect instances. We know people who are truthful, but that does not mean they are perfectly truthful. We know others who are good or beautiful, but they are not perfectly good or perfectly beautiful. These Forms are real and they exist, although in what sense they exist is far from clear.

Everything that we see around us was, for Plato, but a dance of shadows (the play and film called *Shadowlands*, about the life of C. S. Lewis, is based on this idea). True reality lay beyond. The finite world is but a pale reflection of the ultimate reality. The fleeing and changing shadows we see around us do not endure. In Plato's view, the philosopher's task must be to free himself from the cavelike world of sense experience in which he is trapped and to look beyond the darkness of the shadows of the cave which our present world represents to the true reality which can be seen outside it. The body is in a real sense the prison house of the soul. After death my soul, the real me, will, according to Plato, separate from my body and go back to the eternal realm from which it came. Not only will my soul survive death, but it also existed before my birth. When I was born I forgot those things that my soul previously knew. Wordsworth's poem 'Ode to Immortality' (see p. 227) expresses this idea clearly: the young boy grows up and forgets the eternal realm from which he came and to which his soul will return. The different ideas of what it means to talk of a person's soul will be explored in a later chapter.

It is not at all clear how Plato considered the highest Form, the Form of the Good, to be related to the Demiurge. In the *Timaeus* the Forms are described as the thought of the Demiurge, but since the Demiurge used the Form as models after which to fashion the universe, he would seem in some sense to be independent of them. Plato did not seem to feel a need to be consistent on this point, but obviously it was a matter that became of concern to later theologians who did not want anything to be independent of their idea of God.

For Plato, therefore, ultimate reality was timeless and spaceless, beyond any sort of change. The Forms were perfect, not because they were moral agents but because they were metaphysically complete and unchanging. They were perfect as they simply existed – the unchanging exemplars or perfect models of those ideas which we see imperfectly represented in our world. It was an attractive idea and was to have an enormous influence in the development of Christian thought.

Aristotle

Aristotle was born in 384 BCE and died in 322. In 367 he joined Plato's Academy in Athens. After Plato's death he left Athens and was for a time tutor to the young (13-year-old) boy who later became Alexander the Great. He returned to Athens and, failing to be elected as head of the Academy, founded a rival school called the Lyceum to which he attracted some of the Academy's most distinguished members.

Aristotle rejected many of the ideas put forward by his early master, Plato. In particular he moved away from the idea of timeless and spaceless Forms. Plato's thought started from the realm of ideas, with the Forms representing the most truly real of all realities. Aristotle rejected this and considered that ideas only exist in so far as they are expressed in this world. Thus, rather than the Form of the Good existing in its own right, goodness exists only in so far as people are good.

For Plato, every word had its perfect exemplar. Thus a tree is called a tree because it resembles the perfect Form 'treeness' (Plato appears to have considered that every word we use has its own Form – although there is some debate about this). Aristotle, on the other hand, maintained that the form of something is the unchanging element it is. The form of the tree (notice that there is no capital letter for Aristotle's use of 'form') remains unchanged whilst there can be many and various changes in the appearance of the tree. The form of a thing can be considered as its nature, the form is the reason why something is what it is. As will become clear later, Aquinas considered that a human being's soul was the form of his or her body. The form remains the same whilst the human being ages and changes from baby to adult to elderly person. It is the soul as the form of the body which survives death until at some time in the future it is given a new and glorified body.

It was Aristotle who first engaged in the systematic study of logic, and his works on physics and ethics have also had an enormous influence. He maintained that the ideal life for a human being was one of moderation, that nothing should be taken to excess and that virtue always lay between the extremes. As an example, the virtue of courage would lie between the errors of cowardice on the one hand and foolhardiness on the other. 'Moderation in all things' might suitably express this approach (Aristotle's ethics are dealt with in more detail in *The Puzzle of Ethics*, by Peter Vardy and Paul Grosch, HarperCollins, 1999).

Aristotle can be seen, in a way, as combining God with the Platonic Forms. God, Aristotle considered, was the unmoved mover, the timeless and spaceless creator and sustainer of all, on whom the whole of creation depended. God was the one source of all beauty, truth, justice and goodness. This contrasts with Plato, for whom the Forms of Beauty, Truth, Justice and Goodness were apart from the Demiurge who fashioned the universe.

Aristotle defined several different senses of the word 'cause'. In particular, he considered that everything must have an 'efficient cause'. The efficient and final cause of the whole universe was God, the unmoved mover.

It was Aristotle who put forward some of the most interesting arguments for the existence of God, and these were to undergo further development at the hands of Christian theologians. For example, since we see things in motion, Aristotle argues, there must be an unmoved mover which set the motion going. Just as the movement of one snooker ball is caused by its being hit by another, and the other's movement is caused by its being hit by yet another, so motion in the world can be explained similarly. However, just as there must be someone to set the first snooker ball rolling, so too, Aristotle considered, there must have been an unmoved mover who set going all motion in the universe. We see causes that operate within the universe – so there must have been a first cause that was not caused by anything else if we are to explain subsequent causes.

In the early years of the Christian Church's development, Aristotle's philosophy was treated with some suspicion and that of Plato tended to be preferred, chiefly because it was thought that

Aristotle's ideas inevitably led to a materialistic view of the universe. In addition, the early Fathers were strongly influenced by Plato, so there was a tendency for Aristotle, who was seen to be his main rival, not to be taken seriously. In the sixth century Boethius defended Aristotle's approach, but for hundreds of years after this Aristotle's writings were lost in the West and in some cases they were condemned by successive popes. Eventually his works were reintroduced from the East, where they had been preserved by Islamic scholars and had greatly influenced their theology and philosophy. Aristotle was to become the major influence on St Thomas Aquinas and later Catholic philosophy and theology.

It will be readily apparent how attractive the idea of the timelessness and spacelessness of God was to be to later Christian theologians. They wished to hold that God was the creator of all, that the whole of creation depended on God and that God was the source of all life, goodness, justice, truth and beauty. The philosophy of Plato provided the ideal means of expressing these insights and, later, Aristotle's philosophy was used to explain and refine the understanding of religious language.

The biblical approach

The God pictured in both the Old and the New Testaments appears to be anthropomorphic. Although the highest heaven cannot contain God, yet God can walk in the garden with Adam, God can wrestle with Jacob and he can blow with his nostrils to part the Red Sea. God can also change his mind – for instance, in Genesis chapter 18 Abraham persuades God not to destroy Sodom for the sake of first 50, then 45, then 40, then 30, then 20 and finally 10 just men in the city. Chapter 6 says:

Yahweh saw that the wickedness of man was great on the earth, and that the thoughts in his heart fashioned nothing but wickedness all day long. Yahweh regretted having made man on earth and his heart was grieved. 'I will rid the earth's face of man, my own creation,' Yahweh said, 'and of animals also, reptiles too and the birds of heaven, for I regret having made them.'

Here Yahweh regrets having made human beings. It is as if God did not know, when he created them, what they would do. God talks to the prophets and had favourites on no very clear grounds. The 'chosen people', Israel, were not selected because they were an especially virtuous, kind or loyal people. The central image, therefore, is of a God who acts and reacts, of a personal God, intimately involved in the fortunes of his people.

As well as this image, however, the Old Testament also emphasises the unknowable character of God. God cannot be seen, no one can see God and live. God's name is never to be spoken and God is above all earthly images. In Islam this strand of Old Testament thinking is still taken very seriously and no picture or statue of God is permitted in any mosque; generally walls are instead decorated with beautifully patterned tiles. Any attempt to capture God's glory or God's reality by means of an image would, the Israelites thought, debase him and would be idolatry. They were very clearly aware of the difference between their God and the idols worshipped by the people amongst whom they lived. What is more, God was held to be omnipresent, that is, God was present everywhere. The Psalmist puts it this way:

If I ascend to heaven, thou art there! ...
If I take the wings of the morning
and dwell in the uttermost parts of the sea,
even there thy hand shall lead me
and thy right hand shall hold me (Psalm 139:8-10).

And wilt God indeed walk upon the earth?
Behold, Heaven and the highest Heaven cannot contain thee
(1 Kings 8:27).

In the Old Testament we see God only gradually revealing God's nature to God's chosen people, and yet God is a God whom they can to some extent understand.

The New Testament continues and accentuates the anthropomorphic image. God is likened to a Father and to a Shepherd; God speaks directly to Jesus; angels come down from heaven and go up again; there is joy in heaven over one sinner who repents; there are mansions in heaven and wine is drunk; someone who has seen Jesus is held to have actually seen the Father. God is, above all, personal and loving. God is an agent who acts in the world.

The picture of God that emerges from the Bible is, therefore, one of a God who can be seen in some ways as a glorified human figure into whose presence human beings come after death, as if they were coming into the presence of a mighty earthly king. To be sure, the Bible is also aware of the danger of taking this anthropomorphism too far and, particularly in the Old Testament, emphasises the transcendence of God. The Bible never reduces God to a figure like the Greek gods on Mount Olympus or the Norse gods in Valhalla. The biblical God, unlike Plato's Demiurge, creates the universe *ex nihilo* (from nothing) – God 'utters' the world into existence. God says, 'Let there be light,' and there is light.

The early Church

The Church Fathers lived in a world where the many Roman state gods were very like human beings indeed. Deceased emperors were deified and some were worshiped as gods while still alive. One reason why the early Christians were so persecuted was that they refused to take part in this worship.

The Church Fathers knew that their God was above all other gods, that God was the source of everything and that the universe depended on him. They knew that God was eternal – but what did this mean? As will become clear, there are two different meanings of the word eternal, and the early Fathers had to choose between them. When they sought to explore ways of understanding God and of talking about God, the philosophy of Plato was ready at hand and provided the ideal vehicle. So they decided that to talk of God being eternal was to say that God was outside time. The alternative would have been to consider God as everlasting – in other words, within time.

A God who was timeless and spaceless, like Plato's Forms, and who was the source of all motion and the cause of all causes, like Aristotle's Unmoved Mover, was clearly far above all lesser gods. No other god could compare with such a reality. If God had been within time, then the problem would have arisen that there would be something (time) outside of God which God had not created. God would not, then, be the creator of everything, since God would be subject to time. The Church Fathers also wanted God's life to have a quality different to that of our lives. God's life could not just be longer than human life. If God were within time, it would be true that God would endure longer than us, but the quality of God's life would not be radically different. Timeless existence, however, is a different dimension altogether. The Bible talks of God as being eternal. This is partly to draw a contrast between God and mere idols which are made and can be broken – they are transient, whilst the biblical God is far above such limited ideas.

Once one has accepted the idea that the truly perfect, the most ultimately real, must be that which does not change in any way, then the idea of God's timelessness is a logical step. A God outside time could not only create everything in time, but could also be *omniscient* (God could know everything). Timeless God could know the past, the present and the future simultaneously – all times would be present to such a God. This idea has the highly attractive implication that the future is as much present to God as the past, so God knows exactly what the future holds for each of us and God's purposes are assured. This means that God's care for us will never be limited by lack of knowledge of what the future might bring. However, this raises the question of whether, if God sees our future, we can really be considered to be free. We shall have to return to this later.

There may be significant advantages in the idea of a timeless God, if certain scientific discoveries about the origins of the universe are to be taken seriously. We now know that the universe came into existence with the 'Big Bang'. Time and space did not exist before the Big Bang; they started when the universe began. We do not know exactly what happened in the first few thousandths of a second after the Big Bang occurred. Thereafter the course of events is fairly clear. Dense matter exploded apart at enormous velocity, and this matter became the 'stuff' and energy out of which the universe was made. Ever since then the universe has been expanding outwards at close to the speed of light in every direction. If time began with the origin of the universe, the idea of a timeless God would seem to make a good deal of sense. However, advocates of the everlasting God could claim that God's existence pre-dated the Big Bang and that time also existed, measured by reference to the thoughts of this God.

Although the idea of a timeless God is difficult to imagine, St Augustine suggested that it might be approached in this way:

1 Take time and extend it without end in both directions. We then have time that is everlasting, without beginning and without end.

2 Now take this whole time series and roll it into one, so that God has 'the complete possession of eternal life all at once' (Augustine) or 'the whole, simultaneous and complete possession of eternal life all at once' (Boethius).

All times are simultaneously present to the timeless God. There is no before or after for God, there is no future or past. Instead past, present and future are equally present all at once. Augustine gives us a picture which can help us to imagine this. Think of someone sitting on the top of a mountain and looking down on a road that leads past it. On the road are various people. To those on the road, some people will appear to be in front of them and others will appear to be behind, but to the observer on the mountain all appear simultaneously. So it is with timeless God looking down on the road of time. We are in time, so to us some things are in the past (our birth or our great grandparents' death), others are in the future (the birth of our grandchildren) whilst others are in the present (you reading this chapter). To timeless God, however, who looks down on the whole 'road' of time, all times are equally present.

This was an attractive picture and it emphasised the transcendence of God. The view was to be developed by St Thomas Aquinas and remains normative for Roman Catholic theology through to the present day. It does, however, suffer from real problems, and we shall have to examine these in the next chapter.

Summary

There were two main strands of thinking which influenced the early Church Fathers:

1 The Platonic idea that the truly real and truly perfect (the Forms) must be completely unchanging and therefore timeless and spaceless. The Aristotelian, modified version of this maintained that the First Cause or Prime Mover was timeless and spaceless. This led to the idea of God as being beyond time and spaceless.

2 The individual, personal view of God which appeared to be the one put forward in the Hebrew and Christian Scriptures.

Bringing these two strands together was not easy. The real question was, which strand should be given precedence, which view should be allowed to interpret the other? The two views have been held in uneasy tension throughout the history of Christian thought, and it is a tension which is frequently difficult to resolve. Understanding God is like understanding the most difficult of all puzzles, a puzzle which we cannot see, which may be beyond time itself and which we can only dimly comprehend. One of the main purposes of this book is to suggest how different ways of understanding God may be fitted together and their consequences.

In the next chapter we shall see that what it means to talk of God depends to a great extent upon which of the two views above one decides to give priority to.

Questions for consideration

a) Why was Plato's philosophy such a great influence on early Christianity?
b) Do you think Plato's idea of God conflicts with biblical ideas? Why?
c) What are the major differences between Plato's and Aristotle's approaches to philosophy?
d) Do you consider the straightforward biblical view, or the approach of Plato or Aristotle to God to be more compelling?
e) Could God 'regret' having made the earth (Genesis 6) if this is understood in the way we normally use the word?

SECTION 2

DIFFERENT MODELS
OF GOD

FOUR

The Wholly Simple God – a Realist View

The simplicity of god

In the last chapter we saw that for the early Church Fathers, it appeared obvious that God must be timeless and spaceless. God, if God is outside space, could not have a body, since bodies were located in space. The Fathers held that God was (a) wholly *simple*: God could not be divided up into parts – God was God, and did not have arms, legs or any other bodily appendages; and (b) totally *immutable*: God was completely unchanging – God could not be other than God. Since time did not pass for God, God could not change from one state to another. God was not a being amongst other beings – God, being wholly simple, was a unity, absolutely unchangeable and to a very large extent unknowable.

Divine simplicity is of great importance but is not that easy to understand. St Thomas Aquinas (1224–74) developed the understanding of God's simplicity and it is at the heart of the Catholic understanding of God. Aquinas followed Aristotle (384–22 BCE) and considered that *matter*, in abstract, is *pure potential*. Every finite thing has both *act* and *potential*. 'Act' relates to the present state of being of a thing whilst 'potential' relates to the potential a thing has to be something other, or in a different state, than it at present is. Examples might include the following:

- I am a human being and I *could* make a cup of coffee
- This is a cat and it *could* catch a mouse
- This is an atom and it *could* be split

The first part of these sentences states what the things are and the second states various forms of potential. All finite things have a huge array of potentialities, although the range of potentialities is not infinite. A human being *can* or *could* go for a walk, swim, learn, die, kill, think, dance, dress, talk, write, etc. but does not have the potential to fly unaided, to lift objects by the power of his or her mind or to travel to the centre of the earth by burrowing with his or her nose.

Water has the potentiality to turn to ice or steam but not to turn into a duck. At one level, the distinction between actuality and potentiality is a matter of definition, but Aquinas considered that the distinctions found in ordinary language reflect real distinctions within things. Note the emphasis on the words 'can' or 'could': these are potential words. They imply unactualised abilities which could be actualised in the future. Potential, therefore, necessarily presupposes time in which the potential can come to actuality. The move from 'could' to 'does' marks a change in the agent.

No finite being can exist without being something definite, in other words being 'actualised'. To the extent that it exists it is actualised. Any thing that is a 'something' is actual, but its existence also implies that it has potential to be other than what it presently is. To be finite is bound up with the potentiality for change which is in turn bound up with temporality and spatiality. Only a finite being can develop and, for instance, acquire more knowledge – knowledge can, after all, only be acquired by a mind that presently lacks this knowledge.

Human beings have the capacity for self-development, self-knowledge, etc., and these are perfections in human beings. The potentiality for these developed states are part of what it is to be a human being. It is better for a human to have this potential than not but, Aquinas considered, it is preferable to be fully developed than to have the potentiality to develop. *For Aquinas, it is better to arrive than to travel.* To put it another way, it is preferable to possess all perfections than merely to have the potentiality to strive towards them.

This gives rise to the idea that there is a hierarchy of reality:

1   At base level is 'pure matter' which is purely potential with no actuality at all. This is simply raw, chaotic matter with no structure or form.

2   Then comes the whole of the finite universe which consists of things which have actuality (since they are made up of matter) and also potentiality.

3   Finally comes God who is pure actuality with no potentiality at all.

On this basis, to have any potentiality at all is, for Aquinas, an imperfection compared with God. Only God has no potentiality since God is pure actuality. It logically follows from this that God must be outside time since time implies temporality and also that God cannot have a body – God cannot be made up of parts. Anything to do with corporeality, temporality and spatiality (all of which imply potential) cannot apply to God. This is what it means to describe God as simple.

However, this raised an immediate problem. If God is indeed wholly simple and therefore spaceless, immutable and omniscient, he is *very* different indeed from any creature found in the universe. Not only is everything within the universe created whilst God is creator; not only is everything in the universe finite whilst God is infinite; not only is everything in the universe spatial whilst God is outside space, but everything in the universe is in time whilst God is outside time! The differences could hardly have been greater. This gives rise to the next problem.

Using language about the wholly simple God

Significantly, the wholly simple God is not an individual, so to talk of such a God as he or she is grossly misleading, as gender could only apply to an individual. In fact, we do not have any alternative most of the time, but this is because of the inadequacies of our language. If you look back over the discussion so far, you will see that talk of 'a simple God' or even 'the simple God', because 'a' and 'the' imply that God is in some sense an individual amongst other individuals.

How, then, can language which is used to describe created, finite, spatial and temporal things in the universe be applied to God, who is uncreated, infinite, spaceless and timeless? All the words we normally use involve categories that do not apply to God. All the verbs we use – for example, loving, acting, thinking, deliberating, reflecting, knowing or even just existing – involve the concept of time. God is so radically different from us that when words are used to talk about God, those words cannot have the same meanings they normally have.

St Thomas Aquinas is probably fairly described as the greatest theologian that the Christian Church has produced, and his primary concern was this problem: how can the language that the Church uses be applied to God, who is so very, very different from us? His greatest achievement was to show that the use of such language with reference to God was indeed justified. There were those who argued for a *via negativa*, claiming that no positive statements could be made about God since if any positive statement was made this would limit God by eliminating its opposite. However, Aquinas rejected this as to accept the *via negativa* involved refusing to use any positive language about God at all. Aquinas was a realist in that he maintained that language about God was true because it corresponded to the reality of God and he believed that it was possible to speak positively about God – however, such positive language was used in a highly specific manner.

Aquinas drew heavily on the philosophy of Aristotle, whose writings had only recently been brought to the Western world by Islamic philosophers who had been studying them for many years, and he combined Aristotelian philosophy with biblical insights. The scholastic approach to philosophy that he founded has dominated Catholic thinking ever since.

Aquinas held that language falls into three categories:

a) Univocal language

Univocal language occurs where words are used in broadly the same sense in different situations. If, therefore, a girl says that she loves her boyfriend, her mother and her dog then, although the word 'love' is being used in different senses in each case and even though the love may differ, nevertheless there is a similarity between the use of the word 'love' in each case.

Aquinas was adamant that univocal language could not be applied to God, as this would mean that God was created, finite, temporal and spatial, like human beings. The wholly simple God cannot be described in the same way as temporal and spacial creatures are described. Univocal language is not an available option.

b) Equivocal language

Equivocal language occurs where the same word is used in two different situations and with totally different meanings. Here are some examples:

1 I fly to Australia and there is a fly in my soup.
2 My bank keeps my money but the river bank is a good place to sit.
3 The bar in the gymnasium is good to swing on and I drink at the bar in the pub.

In these cases, the same word is being used in two totally different ways. If language about God were equivocal, it would have no content whatsoever for us. I may know what a river bank is, but this will tell me nothing whatsoever about a bank that lends money. If there is no connection between our understanding of love and what it means for God to love, then we could know nothing whatsoever about what it means for God to love. Aquinas therefore rejects equivocal language about God as it would be devoid of content.

c) Analogical language

Analogical language occurs where there is some connection between the way words are used in one sense and the way they are used in another. This language is neither univocal nor equivocal. Take the example Aquinas himself uses:

1 The bull is healthy.
2 The bull's urine is healthy.

At the time when Aquinas was writing, doctors considered that they could deduce something about the health of an animal or a person by looking at their urine. This happens today when urine is checked to find out if a person has been taking drugs, has diabetes or if a woman is pregnant. According to Aquinas if doctors examined a sample of urine and found it to be healthy, they could deduce that, since the urine came from the bull, the bull was healthy. The health of the urine was different from the health of the bull, but the two were nevertheless related, since the latter was the source of the former.

Now let us take another example:

1 God is good.
2 Sarah is good.

We have seen that the word 'good', when applied to God, *cannot* mean the same, even on a magnified scale, as it does when applied to Sarah. To say that it can mean the same would be to say that univocal language can be applied to God, and this is not possible. We have no problem in understanding what it means to say that Sarah is good. Sarah is a temporal, spatial creature and our language expresses what it means for her to be good. In addition, we know that there is a connection between Sarah and God. For Aquinas, this connection was established by his 'Five Ways': the five arguments he put forward which he believed showed that it was rational to hold that God existed (we shall look at a derivation of one of these arguments in a later chapter). If God has created all things, then there is a direct connection between God and Sarah, just as there is a direct connection between the bull and its urine.

It is true, therefore, to hold that 'God is good', since God must have, as a minimum, whatever is necessary to produce goodness in Sarah. This, Aquinas held, is *analogy of attribution*. However, this does not mean that God's goodness is like Sarah's. God is not a moral agent; God has no potential – God's goodness, whatever this is, explains the goodness of Sarah but that is as far as we can go.

Brian Davies OP has an excellent example which puts this clearly:

1 The baker is good.
2 The bread is good.

The baker is a good baker because he makes good bread and the bread depends for its existence on the baker. The bread is good because it is crusty and tasty – but to say that the baker is good does not mean to say that the baker is crusty and tasty!

There is, however, another type of analogy: *analogy of proportion*. Aquinas considered that all species of creatures were created with their own natures. Thus seagulls, cats, horses, wombats, human beings and angels all have their own distinctive natures, and God's nature is distinctive as well. What it means for a seagull to be a good seagull, for a cat to be a good cat, for a person to be a good person and for God to be a good God is different in each case.

When we say something is good, we say it is good in accordance with the nature of what it is to be that thing, so

- for a seagull to be perfectly good, means that it is perfectly whatever it is to be a seagull;
- for a wombat to be perfectly good, means that it is perfectly whatever it is to be a wombat;
- for a human being to be perfectly good, means that it is perfectly whatever it is to be a human being; and
- for God to be perfectly good means God is perfectly whatever it is to be God.

In the case of the first three of these examples, they can all 'fall short' of what it is to be the thing in question. They all have potential and they need not be perfectly good. A seagull can have a missing eye, a wombat can miss a leg, a human being can be morally or physically defective. God, however, being wholly simple, timeless and space-less, *cannot be other than what it is to be God*. God must, therefore, be perfectly good – but this means no more than saying that God must be perfectly whatever it is to be God, it tells us nothing at all about what it is to be God. The content of the statement is very limited. Above all, to say that God is perfectly good does not mean to say that God is a moral agent: God is not good as we are good. First of all, Aquinas rejects the idea that God is a moral agent since there is no standard of morality independent of God, and secondly, God, being wholly simple, cannot be other than God is. To say that 'God is good' means, therefore, that God is metaphysically perfect: God is perfectly whatever it is to be God and, under analogy of proportion, it means no more than this.

The great achievement of Aquinas' theory of analogy was to show how language can truthfully be applied to God. But there is a very heavy price to be paid. *We can say that language about God can truly be applied to God, but we do not know what this language means when it is so applied.* The most we can say is that

1 under analogy of attribution, God has whatever it takes to create goodness in, for instance, seagulls, wombats and human beings – but we do not know what it is for God to be good in this way; and

2 under analogy of proportion, it is true that God is good in what-ever way it is appropriate for God to be good in that God is perfectly what it is to be God. We do not, however, know in what way it is appropriate for God to be good.

Aquinas firmly believed that God existed, but he was profoundly agnostic about the nature of God. Aquinas held that we can know *that* God is, but not *what* God is. We cannot know God's nature, we cannot know what God is like in God's nature or essence. We cannot know what it is for the wholly simple God to exist; still less can we know what it is for that God to create, love or suffer. We can know that God is neither in time nor in space: we can know certain negative things about God. It cannot be emphasised strongly enough, however, that although it is *true* on this view that God loves, acts, creates and is good, we do not know what these terms mean when they are applied to God.

This is a consequence that most people will find very surprising. If you ask a Catholic layperson what it means to say, 'God loves me,' they will in all probability say that this means that God, who is a Spirit, loves them like a father loves his children, only more so. In other words, the assumption will be that univocal language can be applied to God. Catholic theology firmly denies this. It is without doubt true that God loves us, but we do not know what it means for God to love us.

d) Metaphor

Analogy can show how language can truthfully be applied to God, but there is very little content. The better way of speaking about the wholly simple God may be by way of metaphors. Christianity has a rich hoard of metaphors to draw on when speaking of God. God is a mighty king, a rock, a vine, a shepherd, a hen, a fortress. The great strength of metaphors is that no one takes them literally – if a person says, 'God is my rock', no one is foolish enough to ask 'limestone or sandstone?'

Janet Martin Soskice provides an excellent description of the use of metaphors. Soskice is a realist, but a realist of a particular kind as she rejects what she terms *naive realism*: that language about God can be understood in the same way as other human language. A naive realist would claim that a statement like 'God is angry' or 'God walks in the garden' should be understood in exactly the same way as if God were a human being. This, Soskice considers, is ludicrous. God, being wholly simple, cannot have moods or walk in the garden. Effectively, she joins Aquinas in rejecting univocal language. Soskice instead argues for *critical realism*.

The critical realist claims that the best way of speaking of God is through the use of metaphors and that metaphors do, indeed, *refer* to God but they do not *describe* God. They are ways of gesturing towards the transcendent God and they are helpful in doing so, but they cannot be reduced to univocal language. To speak of God as king, rock, vine and shepherd gives some picture of what God is like but stops short of describing God as God is.

Soskice draws parallels between metaphors in religion and metaphors in science. Scientists speak of light as if it is a wave, but light is not a wave. Nevertheless, this can be a helpful way of talking about light. Similarly, God is not a rock or a shepherd, but these ways of speaking may be helpful to the believer in understanding something of what God is. Even in normal language metaphors are used which are rich but are not to be understood literally. To say 'My love is like a red, red rose,' 'She came out of the Head's study with her tail between her legs', or 'He strode into the conference hall all flags flying' may be true (or false) but not literally true.

Metaphors have great strength, but one problem is how one decides which metaphors can truthfully be said to refer to God. For instance, more and more people wish to refer to God as mother as well as as father. How, it may be asked, is one to decide whether this is a true reflection of God's reality or not? Of course, the weight of Church tradition may play a part in this, but merely because metaphors are accepted as true does not mean that they are true in a realist sense. Also the meaning of metaphors may change over time – although these meanings can be learnt. For instance, many would understand what it means to talk of God as shepherd even if they had never met a shepherd.

Summary

Those who hold that the wholly simple, timeless and spaceless creator God exists are realists. They maintain that the statement 'God exists' is true because it corresponds to the existence of a substance which is independent of the universe, which creates it and which can be correctly termed 'God'. It may be, of course, that they are wrong and that no such substance exists, as philosophical realists they would have to be willing to admit the possibility of error. Their language about the wholly simple God is coherent and what they say about this God fits together, but it is not this coherence that makes the statement 'God exists' true.

When we use words about God, these words cannot have the same meaning as when they are used about things or people in the universe. Language about timeless God must be either analogical or metaphorical. The believer can claim that he or she is making true statements about God, without knowing fully what it means for these statement to be true when applied to God.

It follows that when reading the Bible one has to interpret the biblical material with this in mind. Talk of the wholly simple God changing God's mind is metaphorical. The wholly simple God cannot change in any way, since God cannot be other than God is. Talk of God being angry, knowing or loving does not mean the same as when these words are used about human beings. God, being time-less, cannot experience emotions. There are no spatio-temporal mansions in heaven. Heaven is timeless, and there cannot be a heavenly society if there is no time (this is further explored in the chapter on eternal life). God, on this view, cannot suffer, since to suffer is a limitation and cannot apply to God since God is wholly simple. The Bible needs to be interpreted, therefore, by the priest or by the educated person who can understand how its language about God is to be understood in the light of the tradition of the Church.

We shall see in the next chapter that not everyone accepts this view of God. The price paid for God's transcendence is held by some to be too great.

Questions for consideration

a) What does it mean to say that God is wholly simple?
b) Describe what it means to say that the wholly simple God is good.
c) If language about God were entirely equivocal, what would this

mean?

d) Could one have a personal relationship with timeless God?

e) Many metaphors are used to describe God in the Bible. Find two metaphors which involve God, and which you do not think could be meant literally, and explain what you think these mean.

FIVE

The Everlasting, Suffering God – a Realist View

The idea of God being wholly simple, timeless and spaceless arose as a result of the priority given to ideas originating in Greek philosophy. These were seen to be intellectually convincing, and so the biblical, personalist picture of God was interpreted in the light of these ideas. This alternative, personalist approach takes the straightforward language of the Bible more seriously and maintains that God is an individual, personal agent. Certainly God is Spirit, but God is an individual Spirit with whom the believer can have a two-way relationship. God is perfect in this approach, not in the metaphysical sense that applies to timeless God, whereby God is held to be wholly simple, completely immutable and unchanging, but in the moral sense. God is morally perfect in that God's love and care for God's creatures and God's commitment to them will never change.

The view of God as everlasting is the one that tends to prevail in the Protestant churches. One cannot, however, be simplistic about this. Some Baptists, Methodists and Presbyterians may consider God to be wholly simple rather than everlasting, and Anglicans may well be fairly evenly divided. Catholic liberation theologians tend to consider God to be in time. Most believers in all churches have never even thought about the issue! Protestants tend to emphasise the individual's personal relationship with God: the personality of God and of Jesus is at the heart of their beliefs. This does not mean, necessarily, that believers in a wholly simple, timeless God cannot maintain that they have a personal relationship with this God. However, the relationship is difficult to define or envisage, since God can never change, react, respond or love in the way that these words normally imply.

For the everlasting God, time never began and will never end. At some time, God created the universe out of nothing by God's word. At some time in the future, the universe will come to an end, but God will not come to an end. Whether or not there is a universe, God will still exist. God has always existed and will always exist. (Notice that this is not something that can be said about the wholly simple God: the simple God did not exist yesterday and will not exist tomorrow – this God exists timelessly, and so temporal words simply have no application.)

Einstein has shown that time is relative, slowing down as we near the speed of light. This gives rise to the twins paradox. If one twin takes a spaceship at close to the speed of light to the other side of the galaxy and then returns, she may be only ten years older, whilst her twin may have died a hundred years previously. The hymn writer says of God, 'A thousand ages in your sight are but an evening gone.' So, for God, time may not pass as it does for us, but time still passes. One can imagine being in the presence of God and feeling that hardly any time at all has passed, whilst on earth 50 years may have gone by.

Language about the everlasting God can be univocal. Human beings are, indeed, made in the image of God. God can know, be angry, love, remember, change his mind, forgive, and all these words have broadly the same meaning as when applied to human beings. To be sure, God's love is more steadfast and sure than human love; our love grows cold, and the love of God does not. However, what it means for God to love has much in common with what it means for human beings to love. Biblical language can, therefore, be understood in a univocal way.

The heading to this chapter refers to the 'everlasting, suffering God' and the ability of this God to suffer with God's people is of great importance. We have already seen that the wholly simple God cannot suffer as suffering is regarded as a limitation and God has no potential. In recent years liberation theologians, particularly coming from South America, have wished to emphasise that God suffers with the suffering people of the world. Such theologians seek to understand God through the figure of Jesus Christ. When the people of the world suffer, God is held to be with them in this suffering and to be actively involved in this suffering. Just as a human father suffers if his son is in trouble, so God suffers with human beings.

Jürgen Moltmann is one theologian who attempts a response to the problem of evil and, in particular, to the challenge put forward by Ivan Karamazov that the suffering of innocent children can never be justified no matter what end God has in mind (for a discussion of this issue, see *The Puzzle of Evil* by Peter Vardy). Moltmann attempts this response through the figure of Jesus. He maintains that the only way past the protest of atheism against innocent suffering is through a 'Theology of the Cross'. He points to the suffering God who, on the cross, can cry out, 'My God, my God, why have you forsaken me?' Moltmann says: 'In this theology, God and suffering are no longer contradictions, as in theism and atheism, but God's being is in the suffering and suffering is in God's being itself, because God is love' (*The Crucified God*, SCM Press, 1976, p. 227).

The 'Theology of The Cross' stems from St Paul but was developed further by Luther (in 1518 in 'The Heidelberg Disputation'). Moltmann maintains that on the Cross Jesus overcomes suffering:

> suffering is overcome by suffering, and wounds are healed by wounds. For the suffering in suffering is the lack of love, and the wounds in wounds are the abandonment, and the powerlessness in pain is unbelief. And therefore the suffering of abandonment is overcome by the suffering of love, which is not afraid of what is sick and ugly, but accepts it and takes it to itself in order to heal it (op. cit., p. 46).

The God who allows suffering is also the God who suffers with God's people. This view of God emphasises that the best picture of God is Jesus who was, according to traditional Christian belief, God himself.

The view of God as everlasting is highly attractive because it overcomes the difficulties involved in using analogical language about God. The personality of God is emphasised and the understanding that emerges is close to that held by many ordinary believers. However, this approach suffers from four major problems:

1 The everlasting God can be held to be too anthropomorphic and not sufficiently transcendent. Such a God, it may be argued, is rather like a superhuman. God is too finite and insufficiently different from man to be worthy of worship.

2 The everlasting God cannot be said to have created time, since time has always existed, even before the creation of the universe.

3 For the wholly simple God, past, present and future are simultaneously present. The whole of the future is as much present to this God as is my writing this book, your reading it or the extinction of the dinosaurs. To the everlasting God, however, the future is future. The everlasting God is in time and to God, as to us, the future has not yet happened. It may therefore be held that the everlasting God's omniscience is too restricted.

4 The idea of a God who suffers may be held to be a limitation on God. God may be held to be a risen God, a transcendent God, not a God who is so limited that God suffers as we do.

The first point is not an easy one to answer. Much depends on what one considers an adequate model for God to be. Some have held that a wholly simple God who cannot change and cannot be other than God is, is a lesser reality than a God who is an infinite, everlasting Spirit. There is no easy way of deciding the issue.

Process theologians, who are influential particularly in the United States, hold that not only is God in time, but God is also affected by the universe, and needs it in order to develop and grow. Through God's interaction with God's creation God changes. God and the world are closely linked, and changes in the world create real changes in God. Process theology emphasises God's relationship with creation and the centrality of God's love for his creatures. God and the universe are interdependent. God suffers, loves and develops by interacting with the people God has created. All relationships entail development and, if God can enter into relationships with individuals, it necessarily follows that God changes as the relationship progresses. Instead of the traditional Catholic concept of God as 'Being', process theologians emphasise God's 'Becoming'.

Traditionally, Christians have wanted to reject the interdependence of the world and God, since they have held that God created the universe from nothing, whilst God without the universe is fully God. Those who accept that God is everlasting could accept this view without going the way of the process theologians, who affirm the interdependence of God and the world. There is no need to take the everlasting model of God as far as the process theologians wish to take it. The extent to which a God who is in time can develop and change is on a sliding scale, and legitimate debate about that scale is possible.

Advocates of the everlasting model of God can reply to the second question raised above by saying that time is not a thing. Before the creation of the universe, with its physical objects which could provide a measure of time, time would still have existed, since God's thoughts would have been sequential. Because God could think, because God's thoughts were temporal, time would still have existed. Time has always existed because God has always existed. This in no sense makes time into a 'thing' which is external to God.

The third point can be dealt with by saying that God knows everything that it is logically possible to know. God knows the present and perfectly recalls the past. God is *omnipresent* or present everywhere. God's presence is not confined to a particular place: 'If I take the wings of the morning and flee to the uttermost ends of the earth, you are there ...' (Psalm 139:9-10). Because of this God can know what is happening in every corner of the universe, and what has happened in their different pasts. God cannot, however, know the future, as the future has not yet happened. There is not yet any future to know. In a later chapter the whole topic of God's knowledge is dealt with in some detail.

The fourth point may be dealt with by saying that love is held to be at the very centre of the nature of God. According to Franciscan theology a relationship of love between the three persons of the Trinity overflows causing the creation of the universe. A God of love, it may be held, is also a God who suffers because of the failure of people to recognise what is in their own best interests. Matthew's Gospel puts the point like this:

'Jerusalem, Jerusalem, you who kill the prophets and stone those sent to you, how many times I yearned to gather your children together, as a hen gathers her young under her wings, but you were unwilling!' (Matthew 23:37).

Suffering, on this view, far from being seen as a diminution of God may be seen as directly linked to the love of God.

The view that God is an everlasting Spirit and that univocal language can be used about God is probably the most widespread amongst ordinary believers who are not philosophically or theologically trained. They maintain that in prayer an I/Thou relationship with God is possible. Such believers see their relationship with God as being on much the same lines as a relationship between two individuals – although, obviously, God cannot be seen. However, while this is the most common view, we must recognise that truth is not always decided by the ballot box and that ordinary believers are not necessarily the best guide to an understanding of God's nature.

Summary

Those who maintain that God exists everlastingly are realists. They maintain that the statement 'God exists' is true because it corresponds to the existence of an incorporeal Spirit who can correctly be referred to by the word 'God'. As philosophic realists, they would have to admit that they could be wrong and that perhaps no such God exists. Their talk about this God is coherent and fits together, but it is not his coherence that makes the statement 'God exists' true.

The chief problems connected with the idea of an everlasting God are that such a God may seem too much like a cosmic super-human figure, and that, being in time, God may not be able to know the future. However, believers can apply language to this God in much the same way as they apply it to things in the world – in Thomist terms, univocal language can be used about God.

Questions for consideration

a) Could a God for whom time passes be worthy of worship?

b) Why might it be important to claim that God can suffer?

c) Is it possible for a God who is in time to know the future?

d) If believers talk of having a 'personal relationship with God', what do you think they mean?

e) Select three examples from the Old or New Testaments which seem to show that God is an individual. Could these be inter- preted in any other way?

SIX

God as a Reality within a Religious Form of Life – the Anti-realist View

Anti-realists reject the correspondence theory of truth and argue that it is irrelevant. Indeed, they argue, if religious truth claims depend on correspondence then the most that could be established in this way would be that religious statements are *probably* true and this does not fairly reflect the absolute character of religious belief. The reason they hold this view is that if truth is based on correspondence there needs to be some argument to show that there is a Being or Spirit called God to which 'God exists' corresponds if the statement is to be held to be true – and none of the arguments for the existence of God succeed (we shall be looking at these arguments in later chapters). At the very most, anti-realists hold, the arguments for God's existence show that there *may* be such a God and this is too tentative a conclusion to provide grounds for religious belief.

Religious beliefs, the anti-realists argue, do not rest on argument or evidence. Instead they are held as true within a community. They are the ground rules of a form of life, the framework for a whole way of living and seeing the world.

These positions can be illustrated by reference to various understandings of a statement like 'Mary is a virgin'.

- The naive realist will say that this is true because it describes the state of Mary's body when she died, i.e. she died an intact virgin. If she did not die in this state, the statement would be false.
- The critical realist will maintain that this is true because it is a metaphor to describe Mary's status: perhaps as a pure young

woman who was obedient to God. If she was not obedient to God or if the stories told about her willingness to accept Jesus as a son are not true, then the statement would be false.

- The anti-realist maintains this statement is true because it is accepted as true within the life of particular believing communities. Mary's status during her life or at her death is irrelevant to the truth of the statement. There is, it is held, no evidence at all for Mary's sexual status and such evidence as there is claimed to be comes from stories written many years later. However, the anti-realists maintain that this lack of evidence is irrelevant as the statement is accepted as true within some believing communities and it is this acceptance that makes the statement true.

Truth and meaning are not necessarily connected, but they may be. It can be a different question to ask

1 what it means to say that God exists, and
2 how one knows that God exists is true.

Meaning and truth, therefore, are different and in the religious arena it is important to separate what someone *means* by a religious statement from the separate issue of what makes the claimed statement *true*. The anti-realist challenge to traditional ways of understanding religious claims arose out of the collapse of the verificationist challenge, and it may help to outline this first of all.

The verificationist challenge

Verificationists reject all language about God. They do this not because such talk is false but because it is meaningless. Verificationism arose out of the work of the Vienna Circle, a group of philosophers called Logical Positivists which included the English philosopher A. J. Ayer. The Logical Positivists wished to give a scientific account of language and were influenced by earlier work of the Scottish philosopher David Hume (1711–76). Hume had maintained that all statements could be divided into two types (this is Hume's 'fork' – see quote below):

- *Analytic statements* where the predicate is included in the subject, for instance 'all spinsters are female' or 'triangles have three angles' or 'live bears have bones'. We know these are true by analysing the subject of the sentence, i.e. statements such as 'all spinsters are female' are true by definition.
- *Synthetic statements* are statements where the predicate is not included in the subject, for instance 'all spinsters are happy' or 'all live bears have fur'. Almost always these require verification using sense experience: we have to interview spinsters to determine whether they are happy or not.

Hume put his point with considerable eloquence:

> When we run over libraries ... if we take in our hand any volume of divinity ... let us ask, 'Does it contain any abstract reasoning concerning quantity or number?' No. 'Does it contain any experimental reasoning concerning matter of fact and existence?' No. 'Commit it to the flames then for it can contain nothing not sophistry and illusion'(*Enquiry Concerning Human Understanding*).

The Logical Positivists agreed with this maintaining that analytic statements were necessarily true because of the way words were used and any other statement, if it was to be meaningful, had to be capable of verification. A. J. Ayer put the verificationist challenge like this:

> The criterion which we use to test the genuineness of apparent statements of fact is the criterion of verifiability. We say that a sentence is factually significant to any given person if, and only if, he knows how to verify the proposition which it purports to describe – that is, if he knows what observations would lead him, under certain conditions, to accept the proposition as being true or reject it as being false. (*The Problem of Knowledge*, Pelican, 1956,

ch. 1.)

Logical Positivists reject all talk about God as there is no way of verifying such talk. For instance 'God exists', 'God loves me' or 'Jesus rose from the dead' are meaningless statements as there is no way of verifying them. They are not saying these statements are false; they are saying that they are meaningless. It is as if someone were to say, 'Square circles are green'. This statement is clearly meaningless and the Logical Positivists maintain that the same applies to most religious statements. It was not only religious statements that the Logical Positivists rejected (such as 'There is a heaven and a hell') but also many statements made by philosophers such as 'All human beings are determined' or 'I do not know if you have a mind.'

Effectively the Logical Positivists rejected any idea of traditional philosophy as a search for truth and instead saw it as having the purpose of clarifying meaning. Traditional ways of doing philosophy actually caused the problem which philosophy, as correctly practised (at least as the Positivists saw it!), should actually bring to a halt. Positivists maintained that philosophy should be *therapeutic* by stopping people answering questions which should not be asked in the first place.

Anthony Flew turned the verification principle round by saying that unless a statement could be *falsified* the statement would be meaningless. He held that a statement like 'God loves me' is meaningless because the believer will allow nothing to count against this statement. The believer could watch her husband and children die in great pain, could see all her possessions destroyed, could catch an incurable disease, could have all her prayers unanswered and yet still maintain, 'God loves me.' Flew puts it clearly: 'What would have to occur or to have occurred to constitute for you a disproof of the love of, or of the existence of, God?' (Anthony Flew, 'Theology and Falsification', in Flew and MacIntyre, *New Essays in Philosophical Theology*, SCM Press, 1955, p. 96).

His claim is that if nothing will count against a statement, then the statement is not saying anything at all and is meaningless. 'God exists' is rather like saying 'Boojum exists but I do not know what this means and I can give no conditions that would falsify it' (to borrow partly from Anthony Flew and from Lewis Carroll's 'Hunting of the Snark').

Both verificationists and falsificationists were initially seen as posing a real threat to religious language. This threat only diminished when it was shown that

- The verificationists' principle could not itself be verified by their own criteria. In other words, if the verification principle is accepted, then the principle itself is meaningless! Similarly the falsificationist principle would be meaningless as nothing would count against it. It 'dissolves in its own acids'.
- The verificationist and falsificationist principles proposed a new way of understanding meaning: since this threatened the whole basis of religious language, why should the believer accept it?
- Science can today infer the existence of things although there is no direct evidence for them. This applies to fundamental particles, black holes and the like. Verificationists and falsificationists cannot admit some scientific statements are meaningful without also accepting that religious language is meaningful.

John Hick also replied to the verificationists with his theory of *Eschatological Verification*. Religious statements, he held, were meaningful even if the verificationist principle was accepted, because after death religious statements would be verified. Take an example: Verificationists would accept that a statement like 'There are green worms on a planet circling Alpha Centurae' is meaningful because one could state what would verify the statement (namely if we sent a spaceship to the planet and saw the green worms). Similarly, maintains Hick, 'God exists' will be verified after death when we will (or will not) come into the presence of God.

Verificationists and falsificationist basically operated with science as their ideal model and tried to analyse language as if it were a form of mathematical symbolism. Wittgenstein showed that this whole approach did not work. In fact, it was Wittgenstein's later work, more than anything else, that undermined the verification principle.

Wittgenstein

Wittgenstein is probably the most influential philosopher of the twentieth century, even though there are many different opinions about what exactly he was saying. His work can broadly be split into two periods: that of the early Wittgenstein including the *Tractatus*, and the later Wittgenstein who wrote *On Certainty and Philosophic Investigations*. The latter is not an easy book to read, as it is a series of points whose connections are not always obvious. Wittgenstein wanted to make his reader work at understanding him, and whilst this is laudable, it does mean that opinions can differ as to the meaning of his writings.

In his later work, Wittgenstein was concerned with how language is used. Language, he maintained, is a public affair, the idea of a private language does not make sense. Language is also dynamic, and words can have many meanings. The same word or phrase can mean different things in different situations. Nowhere is this more true than in the area of religious language.

Wittgenstein saw the inadequacy of the Logical Positivist approach and, in contrast to his early days, when he wrote the *Tractatus*, came to have a more modest view of philosophy. He regarded philosophy as being a second-order activity which must leave everything as it is. The objective of philosophy was to understand, not to lay down what could and could not be said (which is what the verificationists and falsificationists wished to do).

For more than two thousand years philosophers have sought foundations for knowledge. They have sought some indubitable foundations for all claims to know because, they thought, unless these foundations existed we could not claim to know anything at all. Rene Descartes and John Locke are two of the most influential philosophers in this tradition – they both held that knowledge must have foundations although they differed on what these foundations should be. Descartes set out to doubt everything in order to arrive at something he could not doubt, hence *Cogito ergo sum* (I think therefore I am) and on this foundation and the certainty that came from the clarity of ideas in the mind he built up the whole edifice of knowledge. John Locke believed that the foundations for knowledge were based on sense experiences. He was an *empiricist*: he believed that the final arbiters of certainty were those things which could be experienced. St Thomas, one of Jesus' apostles, was also an empiricist when he said, 'Unless I see in his hands the print of the nails, and place my finger in his side, I will not believe' (John 20:25). Both Descartes and Locke in their different ways, therefore, held that knowledge rested on indubitable foundations. Wittgenstein challenged this whole way of looking at knowledge and denied that there were any indubitable foundations at all.

Instead of knowledge having indubitable foundations, Wittgenstein claimed we are each educated into a particular form of life. We grow up into a certain way of looking at the world. This form of life, this way of looking at the world, is given expression in our language. Language expresses a form of life. When we claim to know something, this is a claim to an achievement, and it requires justification. In order to show that I know how to fly an aeroplane, I would have to demonstrate that I could fly – for instance, by producing my pilot's licence or by getting into an aeroplane and flying it. However, the most basic claims made by language are not justified; they are groundless. This needs some explanation.

In *On Certainty* Wittgenstein discussed G. E. Moore's famous paper 'In Defence of Common Sense'. Wittgenstein showed that language makes contact with the world by certain banal, obvious statements which are groundless. These statements are not justified and do not require justification: there are no grounds for holding them. Statements like 'This is a hand,' 'There is a bookcase' and 'This is a chair' are learnt at our parents' knees and *it simply does not make sense to doubt them*. We cannot justify the claim 'This is a hand' in the sense that it is a groundless belief, a belief held without grounds to support it. We were simply educated into calling certain things hands, bookcases and chairs. If anyone in our society seriously doubts that what you are sitting on is a chair, then there is something wrong with him or her! We learn these groundless beliefs when we are a year or two years old, they are learnt at our parents' knees.

As Norman Malcolm says, it is hard to appreciate the extent to which our most basic beliefs are groundless. By this he means that because we take so many things for granted (such as bookcases, hands and tables) it is difficult for us to appreciate that these are 'obvious' just within the form of life or culture in which we have grown up and been educated.

Nowhere is the groundlessness of our beliefs greater that in the case of religion. The believer believes in God because he or she is brought up within a framework where this belief is accepted or, perhaps, because they converted at a later stage in life and received instruction on what is believed by a particular religious grouping. Just as we learn about tables and chairs at our mother's knee, and these basic propositions are groundless, so belief in God, advocates of this view hold, does not rest on evidence or grounds. Instead, we are educated into a form of life. This is why, it is claimed, religious believers stress so strongly the education of young people – as they want young people to share the same belief structures as their parents. The Catholic or Muslim parent wants their children to go to a Catholic or Muslim school, youth club, etc. so that they can be correctly instructed in the truths of the faith. For the anti-realist, what is 'correct' and what are 'the truths of the faith' are not determined by independent enquiry but by what is accepted within the respected form of life.

One form of life cannot judge the way language is used in another. Scientific ways of using language cannot, for instance, judge religious language. Wittgenstein (writing during the Second World War) asks us to imagine one person saying to another:

1 'I believe there is a German aeroplane overhead.' The reply is:
2 'Well, possibly.'

Then we are asked to contrast this with

1 'I believe there is a Last Judgement.'
2 'Well, possibly.'

Whilst, 'Well, possibly' is a sensible reply to the first belief claim, which is tentative in nature, it is not an appropriate reply to the second belief claim. Belief in the Last Judgement is a belief of a different order and magnitude to that of the first belief. Instead of a tentative belief it is one which shapes the whole of the way a believer looks at the world.

Take another example. Imagine a believer saying: 'I am in pain. This is a punishment for sin. Don't you agree?' Wittgenstein says that he would be unable to answer either 'Yes' or 'No'. When he thinks of pain, he does not think of sin. His mind does not work like that. He does not use ideas like sin to make sense of his world.

One form of life may, therefore, not be able to understand another, and it certainly cannot judge another by its own terms. The non-believing scientist may hear the Catholic believer saying, 'This is the blood of Christ.' If the scientist then grabs the consecrated wine, rushes to her laboratory and carries out an analysis for the presence of blood, she has failed to understand how religious language works. It is more complicated than that. As Wittgenstein puts it: 'For a blunder, that's too big.'

Time and again, when one society meets another, it will judge the other on its own terms. The Westerner meeting the Indian tribe which decides whether a man and a woman should get married by looking at the entrails of a chicken, or which carries out rain dances every year, is likely to dismiss these practices as superstitious and nonsensical. Similarly, the scientist will dismiss the Catholic's claims – and in so doing almost certainly misunderstand them. The more we study tribal societies, the more depth and profundity we find there. If we would understand their way of life or the way of life of Catholic believers, we must study their forms of life as entireties. We must see what role is performed by talk of rain dances or of the blood of Christ. We must seek to understand how their languages express their forms of life.

It is rather like someone watching a game when he or she does not know the rules. If an Englishman watches a game of Australian Rules football, it may at first seem incomprehensible, but after a time he may come to appreciate the rules according to which the game is played. So the non-believer should seek to understand how believers use language, how their language expresses their form of life. The term 'language' concerns not just the words used but also the beliefs, practices and rules associated with a form of life. Wittgenstein talked of language games, but the word 'games' can be misleading and can wrongly trivialise the point Wittgenstein wished to make. He was saying that if we are outsiders to a form of life and to the language with which this form of life is expressed, we must seek to understand the rules by which the language works. One form of life cannot judge another on its own terms.

Wittgenstein's contemporary followers use his ideas (although it is arguable whether or not they accurately reflect his own views!), and their thinking is growing in significance and importance. In terms of sheer volume and scope of writing, the books by Dewi Phillips are notable (cf. particularly *Faith after Foundationalism*, Routledge, 1988). They are influential and generally easy to read. Don Cupitt is certainly the best-known revisionist of traditional Christianity in the anti-realist camp. His books are also easy to read and his arguments are attractive. However, he is not as directly influenced by Wittgenstein as Phillips is, and so I have not dealt with his approach here. However, to those who find anti-realism attractive, Don Cupitt's books are worthwhile reading. A list of some of Phillips' and Cupitt's writings is given at the end of this book. A lesser-known figure is a Dominican priest, Fr. Gareth Moore, whose book *Believing in God, a Philosophical Essay* (T. & T. Clarke, 1989) sets out what he considers Christianity to involve when Wittgenstein's approach is taken seriously.

Moore's book ends with the key statement 'People do not

discover religious truths, they make them.' This expresses his position clearly. A realist would say the opposite. A realist claims that people do not make religious truths, they discover them. The truth of a realist claim is based on its correspondence to reality. The truth of an anti-realist claim is based on coherence: 'God exists' is true, not because the word 'God' refers to an everlasting or timeless substance, but rather because the phrase 'God exists' has a use and purpose within the form of life of the believing community.

If we look at a Christian community (or indeed a Muslim, Hindu, Sikh or Jewish community), then the language that this community uses to talk about its religious beliefs clearly has a value. Religious language gives expression to the religious form of life. The Christian believer considers that God exists; that God is love; that God helps the believer; that Jesus is remembered at or is present in the bread/body and wine/blood of Christ taken at the Eucharist (depending on whether one is a Baptist, Methodist, Presbyterian or Reformed church member on the one hand or a Catholic on the other – Anglicans tend to be divided between the two positions).

The outsider to religion must seek to understand how this language is used. We have already said that rushing off to the laboratory and analysing the Eucharistic wine is a basic mistake, so to understand religious language we must see the role it plays in the lives of believers. 'God is nothing,' Gareth Moore continually says. God is not some individual, some object or some being like Charlie. Aquinas maintains that God is 'no thing': God is timeless substance and is not an individual. However, Moore goes much further than that: his approach is to maintain that God really is nothing. God does, however, exist (like prime numbers exist or the equator exists) as a reality within the form of life of the believing community.

For the believer, God exists, but God does not exist for the non-believer. This is not a dispute about a matter of fact in which one is right and the other is wrong. Rather, it is a dispute about whether terms like 'God', 'prayer' or Last Judgement' have a role in the believer's life.

When one converts from non-belief to belief, one enters a new form of life and one has to learn how the language of this form of life is used. The priest is (says Moore) the 'grammatical expert' who knows how the language of the Church is to be employed. The convert has to undergo instruction or initiation into the new language. The Catholic Rite for the Initiation of Adults (RCIA) might involve, on this view of things, communicating to the convert the truths of the Catholic language game, teaching him the grammatical rules of the Catholic form of life. Within this form of life, some things can be said and others cannot. Catholics are required to assent to certain beliefs, for instance, belief in the assumption of the Virgin Mary and in Papal Infallibility. These claims are true because they cohere or fit in with other Catholic truths, and someone who cannot assent to them cannot be a Catholic.

Catholics (and Muslims, Hindus, Jews, Lutherans, Anglicans, etc.) may be realists or anti-realists. If they are realists they will maintain that the claims held by their faith are true because they correspond or refer to the God who created and sustains the world. In this case they will, as we shall see, need to justify their claim to reference given that there are many alternative belief systems that consider that *their* claims also refer. However, if they are anti-realists, then no claim to reference is required. Instead, statements are held to be true if they are accepted as true within the community of faith.

It cannot be emphasised strongly enough that, in this anti-realist way of thinking, God exists. God really, really, truly, truly exists. But God does not exist as a creator who is distinct from the world: God is not some being who is apart from the world and who sustains it and acts in it. God is instead a reality within the believing community.

Prime numbers provide us with a helpful parallel. To the non-mathematician, prime numbers are not real; they do not exist. The mathematician, however, is in no doubt at all about their existence. If someone learns mathematics, he or she comes to learn about prime numbers; he or she learns about how the language of prime numbers is used. For such an individual, prime numbers become a reality, while previously they were not. Once the individual has seen the reality of prime numbers, nothing can make them unreal to him or her. Mimicking the Psalmist's words, the person might say: 'If I take the wings of the morning and flee to the uttermost ends of the earth, even there prime numbers will be with me,' or perhaps, 'Nothing can separate me from the reality of prime numbers.'

Prime numbers certainly exist – but not in the same way as any being or individual. God is an existing reality, found within the form of life of the believing community, where language about God has meaning and value. Language about God is true, since it coheres or fits in with the other language used by the religious believer.

The importance of community is vital to this view. Anti-realism is community-oriented because it maintains that the reality of God is found and expressed in language and is not independent of language. Since the Second Vatican Council the Catholic Church has heavily emphasised the idea of community. Increasingly, being a Catholic is seen to be to belong to the Catholic community. Community is central. The same is true of the anti-realist approach. It is within the community that God's reality is found, and it is the language of the community that gives this reality expression.

In some ways this view can be seen as a development beyond the idea of a timeless God. It is the result of the progressive process of abstraction that has taken place in human thinking about God. God can no longer, in this view, be thought of as a wholly simple substance or an everlasting Spirit. Instead, the existent reality that is God is found within the believing community. As Jesus said, 'Wherever two or three are gathered together in my name, I will be with them.' The believer, once he or she has come to understand what the term 'God' means, can never be separated from this reality.

Rationally, this approach has many strengths. It does, however, suffer from significant weaknesses as well. It does not take seriously the claim of mystical and religious experiences of a loving creator God. It is also prescriptive in that it lays down what it is that believers are doing. This approach is said to stem from Wittgenstein, and yet it flies in the face of his demand that philosophy should 'leave everything as it is'. Christian believers almost universally *do* believe in a creator God who interacts with the universe and they use this language in a realist sense – even if they are not aware that they are doing so!

In the chapters that follow we shall be exploring the meaning that this approach gives to talk about prayer, miracles, eternal life and other religious terms. Clearly, as God is not, on this view, an agent outside the universe who nevertheless interacts with it, there will need to be some revision of the way in which religious language is understood – but this is, after all, a revisionary view!

Summary

God, in the anti-realist view, really exists. The statement 'God exists' and the religious language that goes with it are true. However, truth is based on coherence within a particular community or form of life. The word 'God' does not refer to some everlasting spirit or timeless substance; God is not an individual. Different truths are being affirmed by different forms of life.

One form of life cannot judge another. The language of science cannot judge that of religion nor can religion judge science. Hindu truths, Muslim truths and Christian truths are all true, but there is no single absolute truth. Truth is relative. The believer, when he or she converts from non-belief, comes to find a use for language about God, where previously that language had no place in his or her life. In finding the value of religious language, the individual finds God. Believers do not discover religious truths – they make them.

Questions for consideration

a) Are there any parallels between the existence of God and the existence of prime numbers?

b) 'If there were no religious believers God would not exist.' How might this view be justified?

c) What is a 'form of life'?

d) Where did you learn about God? How big an influence do you think parents and background have on religious beliefs that an individual may have?

e) What is the difference between saying 'God is nothing' and 'God is no-thing'?

f) What makes religious beliefs true?

THE PROBLEM
OF REFERENCE

SEVEN

The Cosmological Argument

It should by now be obvious that the word 'God' has many meanings. Those who believe in a wholly simple God or an everlasting God maintain that statements about God are true because they correspond to the God who exists independently of anything in the world. Obviously, it will be important for them to show that the creator God exists. After all, many people deny that there is such a God.

If we want to prove that something exists, we first need to know what it is. If I were to ask you to find an aardvark, you might reasonably first want to know what an aardvark is, if you did not it might be exceedingly hard to find one! In many ways, therefore, the sensible starting point when looking at arguments for God's existence would be to consider each of the different views of God that we have so far considered.

In fact, we are not going to work this way round. The reason is that the arguments for the existence of God are well defined and well known in philosophic circles. So we shall start by looking at the arguments, in the case of each considering the view of God to which it points. It is important to recognise that different arguments point to different conceptions of God.

First we shall look at the Cosmological Argument and then, in succeeding chapters, we shall move on to the Ontological Argument, the Design Argument and finally the Argument from Religious Experience.

The term 'cosmological' derives from the word 'cosmos', meaning 'the universe'. The Cosmological Argument is an argument that starts from the existence of the universe and tries to prove from this that God exists. The argument depends on a willingness to ask the question 'Why is there a universe?' After all, the universe exists and it might not have done. If we are not interested in the question, if we just say, 'Well, the universe is just there and that's all there is to it,' then the argument will not get off the ground.

The Cosmological Argument has one tremendous advantage. It starts from an invulnerable first premise which we all accept, the existence of the universe. It is an *a posteriori argument*, an argument that starts from something we experience, in this case the universe. The steps in the Cosmological Argument may be challenged, but its starting point is undoubted.

Natural Theology attempts to demonstrate that 'God exists' is true by showing that the word 'God' successfully refers to that which exists independent of the created universe and on which this universe depends for its existence. Aquinas' Five Ways are the cornerstone of Catholic Natural Theology because they claim to show that language about God successfully refers. Aquinas was not creating new arguments but using old ones. Aquinas' Fifth Way (which is really a design argument) owed much to Plato's argument in the *Timaeus*. There are five arguments:

1 From *Motion*
2 From *Efficient Causes*
3 From *Contingency and Necessity*
4 From *Grades of Perfection in Things*, and
5 From *Design*

It is not certain that Aquinas *did* intend his arguments to establish the existence of God independent of faith. Lubor Velecky maintains that Aquinas was already a firm believer and wrote for a world which accepted Aristotelian categories. He would never have expected the arguments, which he treats very briefly, to have had the weight they have subsequently been given. However, Velecky may not be right and possibly Aquinas *did* intend to produce proofs and, indeed, his whole system depends on their success.

For our purposes the issue is, however, whether the arguments succeed in establishing reference to God, whatever Aquinas' intentions may have been. Possibly the most important argument is Aquinas' 'Third Way'.

a) Aquinas' Third Way. The argument from Contingency and Necessity
Aquinas' argument runs as follows:

> The Third Way is taken from possibility and necessity and runs thus. We find in nature things that are possible to be and not to be, since they are found to be generated, and to be corrupted, and consequently, it is possible for them to be and not to be. But it is impossible for these always to exist, for that which can not-be at some time is not. Therefore if everything can not-be, then at one time there was nothing in existence. Now if this were true, even now there would be nothing in existence, because that which does not exist begins to exist only through something already existing. Therefore if at one time nothing was in existence, it would have been impossible for anything to exist; and thus even now there would have been nothing in existence – which is absurd. Therefore, not all things are merely possible, but there must exist something the existence of which is necessary. But every necessary thing either has its existence caused by another, or not. Now it is impossible to go on to infinity in necessary things which have their necessity caused by another, as has already been proved regarding efficient causes. Therefore we cannot but admit the existence of some being having of itself its own necessity, and not receiving it from another, but rather causing in others their necessity. This is what all men speak of as God.' (*Summa Theologiae* 19.2.3.)

This can be summarised in the following steps:

1   In nature, things can either exist or not exist.
2   If this is so, given infinite time, at some time everything must not-be.
3   If there was once nothing, nothing could come from it.
4   Therefore something must necessarily exist (*note carefully that this is not* God).
5   Everything necessary must be caused or uncaused.
6   The series of necessary things cannot go on to infinity, as there would then be no explanation for the series.
7   Therefore there must be some Being 'having of itself its own necessity'.
8   This is what everyone calls 'God'.

It is important to note that Aquinas' arguments do not aim to move back in a temporal sequence – rather, they seek to establish *dependence* , the dependence of the world on God now. Aquinas believed that there was no way of establishing that the universe had a beginning in time. This was a revealed doctrine. He did, however, believe his arguments established the need for the world to be dependent on God.

Aquinas' argument arrives at 'That which is necessary to explain the universe' or that which is necessary to explain motion, causation or contingency. We do not know what God is, but whatever God is, God is whatever is necessary to explain the universe's existence. There is a jump, however, from whatever this is to describing it as God. This gave rise to Pascal's quotation: 'The God of Abraham, Isaac and Jacob – not the God of the philosophers'. Aquinas ends his proofs by saying, 'This is what everyone calls God' but this may be closer to the 'God of the philosophers' than to the living, loving, suffering God of the Christian tradition. Aristotle's Prime Mover appears radically different from the God of most Christians. If we said that God was 'whatever sustains the universe in existence' we would be somewhere near to what Aquinas was saying, but this 'whatever' may be some way from Yahweh. It is important to recognise that Aquinas ends up with God as *de re* necessary – necessary in and of himself and cause of himself.

Certain features of Aquinas' argument are particularly noteworthy:

1 It starts from what Aquinas considers to be an undeniable fact: that things in the world come into existence and go out of existence (1 above). They are contingent, they depend on something else for their existence.

2 There is a switch from 'can' to 'must' between 1 and 2 above which may be challenged. Aquinas was, of course, not aware of the *Principle of the Conservation of Energy* whereby matter and energy change their state but do not go out of existence. From this, the fact that something goes out of existence does not mean that the matter/energy that made it up ceases to exist. This undermines point 2 above.

3 Aquinas maintains that there can be *caused necessary beings* (5 above). Aquinas was thinking in terms of angelic beings which were dependent, in that they were created but they did not go out of existence, so they were necessary. Copleston (see below) eliminated this stage, and thereby, made the argument simpler.

4 The argument rejects the possibility of an infinite series (6 above) – it claims that there has to be an end to the series of necessary things which are dependent on other necessary things. This point was well illustrated by Stephen Hawking in his book *A Brief History of Time* (Bantam, 1988). On p. 1 he tells of a woman who interrupted a lecture by a scientist on the origins of the universe saying that she knew better. When asked to explain she said that 'the world is really a flat plate supported on the back of a giant tortoise'. The scientist asked what the tortoise stood on and she replied 'You're very clever young man, very clever. But it's tortoises all the way down.' The issue is whether there is a 'necessary tortoise' – in other

words, whether there is an uncaused cause which supports the universe, or whether the series of causes can go on to infinity. Leibniz argues the same point when discussing his Principle of Sufficient Reason.

5   Aquinas 'labels' the uncaused, necessary being on which all else depends as 'God' (8 above) – the last line of four of the 'Five Ways' is, 'This is what all men speak of as God.' He does not argue for the claim and given that Aquinas' God is metaphysically simple, having no body or parts, is timeless, spaceless and wholly immutable, this may be debatable as some hold that personality, love and the ability to suffer with creation are defining features of God and these are features that cannot be univocally applied to Aquinas' God.

6   Aquinas claims to arrive at something which is *de re* necessary (necessary in and of itself). However, this could be the universe itself or it could be God.

7   It may be that the idea of a Necessary Being, is itself misconceived. Both Kant and Hume maintained that only propositions (such as 'all spinsters are female') are necessary. A 'Necessary Being' could be a contradiction in terms.

Leibniz, in his *Theodicy* (written in 1710) put the Cosmological Argument forward as follows:

> Suppose the book of the elements of geometry to have been eternal, one copy having been written down from an earlier one. It is evident that even though a reason can be given for the present book out of the past one, we should never come to a full reason. What is true of the books is also true of the states of the world. If you suppose the world eternal, you will suppose nothing but a succession of states and will not find in any of them a sufficient reason.

Leibniz says that 'the great principle' of the Cosmological Argument is that 'nothing takes place without a sufficient reason'. This is known as the Principle of Sufficient Reason. By a 'sufficient reason' Leibniz means a complete explanation. Thus to explain the existence of one book by saying that it is copied from another or to explain your existence by saying that you were a child of your parents only gives a partial explanation. If there is going to be a complete or sufficient reason for the book or for your existence, we have to get back to something that does not depend on anything else – and this will be God.

Leibniz is saying that if we suppose the world to be everlasting – to go on and on, backwards in time for ever – we will never come to a complete or sufficient explanation for its existence. We should not be satisfied with such an unending regress, he claims, but should instead recognise that the whole universe depends on God, who is uncaused and does not depend on anything else.

The question is, of course, whether we have to accept the Principle of Sufficient Reason. Is it any more improbable that each state of the universe should be explainable by a previous state – going on and on to infinity – than that the universe should depend on an uncaused God? Scientists do now know that if we go back in time to the very beginnings of the universe, time ceases to exist at the moment of the 'Big Bang.' The universe and time itself started with the Big Bang. This, perhaps, may make it less plausible to claim that each state of the universe can be explained by a preceding state. If, as critics of the Cosmological Argument claim, God was not the cause of the Big Bang, they need to suggest what the cause was.

Both David Hume and Immanuel Kant criticised the Cosmological Argument. Hume maintained that we have no experience of universes being made and it is simply not possible to argue from causes within the universe to causes of the universe as a whole. There is a logical jump which the argument fails to recognise. It is one thing to talk about causes that operate within the whole system of the universe, but it is an entirely different matter to speculate about whether the system as a whole is caused. Immanuel Kant rejected the argument outright not only because he maintained that the idea of a 'Necessary Being' was incoherent but also because our knowledge is limited to the phenomenal world of space and time and it is not possible to speculate about what may or may not exist independently of space and time.

b) Copleston's reformulation of Aquinas' 'Third Way'

The Cosmological Argument has been reformulated and put into a more modern form by the leading Jesuit philosopher, Professor F. Copleston (a former Principal of Heythrop College of the University of London). He put his version forward in a debate with Bertrand Russell on BBC Radio in 1947 (cf. *Why I am not a Christian*, Bertrand Russell, Allen & Unwin, 1957, p. 144). His argument is shorter than that of St Thomas Aquinas, although the reasoning is similar to that of Aquinas whilst some unnecessary steps are avoided. Copleston's version can be summarised as follows:

1 We know that there are some things in the world which do not contain within themselves the reason for their own existence.(In other words, there are things in the universe which are contingent or not self-explanatory. They are 'might–not–have–beens' because, like you and I, they might not have existed – if, for instance, our parents had not met.)

2 The world is simply the real or imagined totality of individual objects, none of which contains within itself the reason for its own existence. (Copleston is saying here that everything within the universe is not self-explanatory. He moves from 1 above, in which he claims that some things depend on others, to saying here that all things in the universe depend on other things. All things within the universe can only be explained by some cause or reason external to them.)

3 Therefore, the explanation for the existence of everything in the universe must be external to the universe. (Once we have accepted the second premise, then, *if* we accept Leibniz's Principle of Sufficient Reason – his insistence that there must be a full and

complete explanation – it follows that outside the universe there must be a cause for everything in the universe.)

4 This explanation must be an existent being which is self-explanatory – in other words, a being which contains within itself the reason for its own existence. This Copleston refers to as a 'necessary being'. (If everything within the universe is contingent or dependent, then, if we have accepted 3 above, the final explanation must be necessary – in other words, this final explanation must exist. It could not fail to exist; it is not dependent on anything else. This final explanation Copleston considers to be God.)

Copleston defined a necessary being as 'a being that must and cannot-not exist'. Bertrand Russell responded to Copleston largely by rejecting his terminology. Once you accept the terminology, particularly the claim that everything in the world is either contingent or dependent, then the argument becomes much more persuasive. Once one accepts that everything is dependent upon something else, then it follows that something must be necessary or non-dependent. Russell avoided this by refusing to accept the use of the term 'contingent' or the notion of dependence. He said in reply to Copleston: 'I should say that the universe is just there, and that is all.'

Copleston's response to this is significant. He said:

> If one does not wish to embark on the path which leads to the affirmation of transcendent being, however the latter may be described, one has to deny the reality of the problem and assert that things 'just are' and that the existential problem in question is just a pseudo-problem. And if one refuses to even sit down at the chess board and make a move, one cannot, of course, be checkmated. (ibid.)

As I said at the beginning of this chapter, the Cosmological Argument depends upon a willingness to ask the question 'Why is the universe here?' If one is willing to accept that the universe is just a brute fact, then the question does not get posed and the answer 'God' will not be required.

David Hume argued that it was illegitimate to move from saying that every event in the universe has a cause to the claim that therefore the universe has a cause. Bertrand Russell made a parallel point by remarking that this was rather like moving from saying that every human being has a mother to the claim that the human race as a whole has a mother. It is quite correct to claim that all humans have mothers (or at least that they come from a female egg cell – the advance of fertilisation and embryo research may soon mean that it will not be necessary for a woman actually to carry a baby in her womb, and instead it could be developed in an incubator for the full nine months), but it is certainly not correct to claim that the human race as a whole has a mother. One cannot move from individual causes to a claim that the totality of all has a cause.

Copleston considers we should ask for an explanation of the universe, while Russell maintains that we should not. If we were to push Russell by saying, 'But everything requires an explanation, and so the universe must therefore require an explanation,' and if Russell were then to agree with us (which, given his argument in the previous paragraph, would be unlikely), we might then arrive at God as the explanation for the universe's existence. However, Russell would then be able to turn the table on us by saying, 'If everything requires an explanation, what is the explanation for God?' We could not easily refuse to explain God when we had denied Russell the right to refuse to explain the universe. Why should God be self-explanatory in a way that the universe itself is not? It is this problem that supporters of the Cosmological Argument need to overcome.

Fr. Martin Lee rejects the Cosmological Argument ('Why Is There Something Rather Than Nothing?' *Heythrop Journal*, 1985) because, he maintains, God must be either something or nothing. If God is something, then we can ask for reasons why this something exists, and so the ultimate 'Why' question would not be solved by positing the existence of God. If God is nothing, then God would not be an agent who created the universe. Lee accuses Aquinas of trying to say that God is neither something nor nothing – rather, a special category somewhere between the two. This, Lee maintains, is not a possible position. Lee's challenge is a good one, but it does not necessarily disprove Aquinas' case. Lee uses the terms 'something' and 'nothing' univocally and, as we have seen, Aquinas rejects such use of language. Aquinas would be quite happy to say that God transcends the distinction between something and nothing, and this is exactly what he, Aquinas, is saying. Whether or not this is valid is an open question.

Much is going to depend on personal opinion, and argument is likely to fail at this point. The dilemma can be shown by quoting from two leading philosohers of religion. John Hick, in his book *Arguments for the Existence of God*, says: 'The atheistic option that the universe is "just there" is the more economical option.' Richard Swinburne, in his book *The Existence of God*, says: 'God is simpler than anything we can imagine and gives a simple explanation for the system.' Your decision about which of these two views you favour will determine whether or not you find the Cosmological Argument persuasive. Swinburne's claim that God is a 'simple' explanation needs to be looked at with some care as the very nature of a wholly simple God is highly complex and it is by no means obvious that God *is* a simple explanation.

If the Cosmological Argument succeeds, then the uncaused cause, the unmoved mover, the being having of itself its own necessity, is clearly different from anything within the universe. Nothing within the universe is the cause of itself. Everything depends on something else. As we have already seen, it is very difficult to use language to talk about this wholly simple, timeless God, as this God is so different from us. God is so transcendent and unknowable that although we may be able to use language about God, we cannot really know what this language means. This is a necessary consequence of the wholly simple, timeless God view, and it is the price that supporters of the wholly simple God have to pay for affirming God's transcendence and otherness.

The influence of Aquinas' Five Ways, particularly on Catholic Natural Theology, cannot be overestimated, but their effectiveness as proofs for the existence of God (whether or not Aquinas himself considered them to be taken in this way) is debatable.

c) The Kalam Cosmological argument

Another form of the Cosmological argument is the Kalam Cosmological argument which was first put forward by Islamic theologians and philosophers. Instead of arguing that the universe depends on God now, this arguments sets out to show that God is the originating cause. It can be summarised as follows:

1 Everything that has a beginning of existence must have a cause
2 The universe began to exist
3 The universe has a cause
4 The cause is God

1 is regarded as being intuitively obvious, although it was a position rejected by David Hume who maintained that there is no necessary link between a cause and a supposed effect, the two may just occur together. A ship going through the water may not cause the wake, the wake may occur at the same time as the movement of the ship but without the two being connected. Also, development in our understanding of particle physics indicate that some particles come into existence and go out of existence without a cause, thus implying that there may be random or uncaused events. However, the claim that some events can occur without any cause cannot be established as it is possible that present unknown causes may be found in the future.

2 is held to be supported by the 'Big Bang' theory which holds that the universe originated approximately ten thousand million years ago in an unimaginably vast explosion and at the commencement of this explosion time and space did not exist; there was a singularity from which all matter and energy originated. This can be

challenged because there is no way of showing whether there was or was not some prior state which could explain the universe, none the less it may be held to be plausible even though there are now alternative theories.

3 is held to follow from 1 and 2 whilst 4 is held to be the most plausible cause given 3 – particularly if God can be held to be in some sense personal and to be pure mind rather than matter. Mind may be held to be the best ultimate explanation for matter – although, if God is wholly simple and timeless there are obvious problems with the idea of God being 'personal' or being described as 'pure mind' and one would have to resort to analogical language (see p. 36).

The Kalam argument depends on assumptions that can be rejected, for instance:

- that every event has a cause;
- that the universe needs an explanation outside the universe;
- that the question 'what caused God' is illegitimate; and
- the Kalam argument may be held to point to an originating rather than a conserving cause, and thus to a deist view of God.

Nevertheless, it does point to the fact that we do not know what caused the Big Bang. Such a question may be beyond the reach of science and shows the point at which philosophy must take over. Effectively it labels the explanation for the existence of the Big Bang as 'God'.

Summary

The success of the different versions of the Cosmological Argument depend on a willingness to ask the question, 'Why is there a universe?' If you are content simply to accept that the universe is just there and does not need an explanation, or that it can be explained by an infinite regress, then the Cosmological Argument fails. In addition, God must also be shown to be a simpler or better ultimate explanation than the brute fact of the existence of the universe, and the idea of an uncaused cause which transcends the distinction between something and nothing must be shown to be credible.

Questions for consideration

a) Why might God be considered the best explanation for the existence of the universe?
b) If God created the universe, who created God? Is this a fair question?
c) What might it mean to say that God is neither something nor nothing?
d) What are the chief differences between the Kalam argument and Coplestone's version of the Cosmological Argument?
e) Why might it be held that what the Cosmological Argument arrives at is not the God whom religious believers worship?

EIGHT

The Ontological Argument

The Ontological Argument is totally different from any of the other arguments on several grounds:

1 It does not start from experience as a starting point.
2 It claims to arrive at the existence of God by analysing the idea of God and this idea does not depend on experience – it is therefore an a priori argument.
3 If the argument succeeds, then the existence of God is logically necessary and, as a matter of logic, it simply does not make sense to doubt that God exists.

The key issue in the ontological argument is what is meant by 'necessity'. Once you have understood this you will have begun to understand the argument. Conversely, if you fail to understand this you will not have begun to appreciate what the argument is about.

Take this issue slowly and start by moving back a little. Take the statement 'All bears are animals'. This statement is true, but what makes it true? It is true because we know by examining or analysing the word 'bear' that it must be an animal. It is part of the very definition of the word 'bear' that it should be an animal. It simply does not make sense to say that a bear is not an animal. Once we understand what the word 'bear' means we can see that various statements are true, including

1 All bears will die, and
2 Bears have bones

It will be clear from this that when we are talking here about bears we are referring not to Paddington Bear, Rupert Bear, Pooh Bear or even teddy bears but to bears that are animals, that are born and die and that have sense organs. I am defining what a bear is and the truth of the statement follows from my definition. If I want to determine the truth of these statements I first have to understand what is meant by the word 'bear'.

Now take another statement:

3   All bears are brown

This is different from the previous statement not just because it is not true (we know that there are black bears and polar bears) but because the statement could only be proved to be right or wrong based on *evidence* . We would have to check all the bears we could find to find whether they were all brown and if we found one black or white or red bear the statement would be untrue. To take a distinction we have already referred to, 'All bears have bones' is an analytic statement and 'All bears are brown' is a synthetic statement.

Aquinas maintained that as far as we are concerned 'God exists' is a synthetic statement. It makes sense to say that 'There is no God' just as it makes sense to say 'There are no bears.' Both statements would be based on evidence and both statements may or may not be true. Aquinas did not think it was possible for human beings to know God's essence. If we could know God's essence, then he considered that we would be able to know that God's essence includes God's existence, but we cannot know this. The Ontological Argument maintains that 'God exists' is an analytic statement. It cannot fail to be true. If this is the case, then to determine whether the statement is true we must first begin with a definition of God.

The Ontological Argument effectively starts with the claim that 'God exists' is *de dicto* necessary. *De dicto* necessity is the necessity found in propositions and is based on how words are used (*de dicto* means 'of words'). It is logical nonsense to say that God does not exist since once we have understood what the word God means we could not fail to see that God exists in just the same way as once we have understood what a bear is we could not fail to understand that it is an animal. However, it seeks to move from God's *de dicto* necessity to God's *de re* necessity (that God necessarily exists in and of God's self, that there exists a substance called God that cannot not-exist) – and this is where the problems arise.

Aquinas rejects the Ontological Argument as he holds that we do *not* have an agreed definition of God. Some people even hold that God has a body (which Aquinas considers to be absurd). We cannot, therefore, start from an agreed definition since not only can we not agree on a definition but even if we could we have no way of knowing that this definition is correct. This, then, is where the whole debate starts. If you think that it is odd that no mention has yet been made of the main figures in the debate, then this is because you will not really understand any of them until you have understood that the Ontological Argument is an a priori argument which is held to show that God's existence is *de dicto* necessary and that this can then be used to arrive at God's *de re* necessary existence. If this is accepted, then everything is going to hinge on how you define God.

a) St Anselm's first argument

If everything is going to turn on definitions, it is not surprising that Anselm's first argument starts with a definition. Anselm (1033–1109) defines God as 'That than which nothing greater can be conceived.' Notice that this definition is given in the *Proslogion* in St Anselm's *Basic Writings*, Part 1, (2nd edition translated by S.N. Deane, Open Court, 1974), ch. 2, which is an address to God. Anselm is trying to show how self-evident God's existence is to a believer. Anselm's first argument (in *Proslogion*, ch. 11, ibid.) runs as follows:

Well then, Lord, You who give understanding in faith, grant me that I may understand, as much as you see fit, that You exist as we believe You to exist, and that You are what we believe You to be. Now we believe that You are something than which nothing greater can be thought. Or can it be that a thing of such a nature does not exist, since 'The Fool has said in his heart that there is no God' (Ps. 13, 1; 52, 1)? But surely, when this same Fool hears which I am speaking about, namely 'something-than-which-nothing-greater-can-be-thought' he understands when he hears, and what he understands is in his mind, even if he does not understand that it actually exists. For it is one thing for an object to exist in the mind, and another thing to understand that an object actually exists. ... Even the Fool, then, is forced to agree that something-than-which-nothing-greater-cannot-be-thought exists in the mind, since he understands this when he hears it, and whatever is understood is in the mind. And surely that-than-which-a-greater-cannot-be-thought exists in the mind since he understands this when he hears it, and whatever is understood is in the mind. And surely that-than-which-a-greater-cannot-be-thought cannot exist in the mind alone. For if it exists solely in the mind, it can be thought to exist in reality also, which is greater. If, then, that-than-which-a-greater-cannot-be-thought exists in the mind alone, this same that-than-which-a-greater-*cannot*-be-thought is that-than-which-a-greater-*can*-be-thought. But this is obviously impossible. Therefore there is absolutely no doubt that something-than-which-a-greater-cannot-be-thought exists both in the mind and in reality.

Anselm believes already and this is significant. The *Proslogian* is, effectively, a prayer and not a piece of philosophy, and this is important to bear in mind.

The first version of St Anselm's argument proceeds as follows:

- God is by definition that than which nothing greater can be conceived. This definition is understood by believers and non-believers.
- It is one thing to exist in the mind alone and another to exist both in the mind and in reality.
- It is greater to exist in the mind and in reality than to exist in the

mind alone.

- Therefore God must exist in reality as well as in the mind. If God did not, then we could conceive of one who did and he would be greater than God.

In effect, what Anselm is saying is that 'God exists' is an analytic statement - we can show that the statement is true merely by analysing what it means to be God.

Gaunilo challenged Anselm with his *lost island* argument. Gaunilo asks us to imagine a lost island – an island greater than any that can be conceived to exist. On the basis of Anselm's reasoning, Gaunilo holds, the island must exist. However, Anselm replied to him that Gaunilo had not understood his argument. Anselm's point is that only God has all perfections and his argument therefore only applies to God, only God is 'that than which none greater can be conceived', only God is the greatest possible being. Because God is perfect God must, for Anselm, be necessary, as otherwise God would lack something that belongs to perfection (although it may be asked what characteristics belong to perfection and this may not be clear).

Gaunilo is saying that God is merely the greatest *actual* being just as the island is the greatest *actual* island – but this is *not* what Anselm is saying. Anselm is claiming that God is the greatest *possible* being and his argument only applies to God.

b) René Descartes (1596–1650)

Descartes' version of the argument is in some way clearer than that of Anselm. Descartes holds that just as we cannot conceive of a triangle without it having three angles; just as we cannot think of a mountain without a valley so we cannot think of God without conceiving him as existing. Descartes gave several more precise formulations of his argument in response to the criticism put forward by Caterus, a contemporary. His second restatement is as follows:

1 Whatever belongs to the essential nature of something cannot be

denied of it;

2 God's essence includes existence; therefore
3 Existence must be affirmed of God.

Descartes did take into account the type of attack that Gaunilo made against Anselm's argument. Descartes says:

1 The argument applies only to an absolutely perfect and necessary being. It cannot, therefore, be applied to something like a lost island.
2 Not everyone has to think of God, but if they do think of God then God cannot be thought not to exist (note the significance of this when we examine Malcolm's version of the argument below).
3 God alone is the being whose essence entails God's existence. There cannot be two or more such beings.

Aquinas rejects precisely the point that Descartes wants to affirm. Descartes says we can know God's essence and therefore we can say that God must exist. Aquinas does not think that God's essence is knowable to us.

In a way right Descartes is right. It is impossible to have a triangle without it having three angles, just as it is impossible to have a spinster who is not female. The predicates follow from the subject. However, all this tells us is something about the *idea* of a triangle and not about whether there are any triangles. We might say that 'It is necessary for a unicorn to have a horn' and this may indeed be true, but this does not prove there are any unicorns.

c) Kant (1724–1804)
It was Kant who called this the 'ontological argument', as he thought that the argument made an illegitimate jump from ideas to *ontos*, 'reality'. Kant held there were various objections to the argument:

1 We have no clear idea of a necessary being. God is defined largely

in negative rather than in positive terms

2 Necessity, Kant held, applies to propositions (like triangles have three angles) and not to anything in reality. There are *no* necessary things.

3 It is true that a triangle must have three sides or a unicorn must have a horn but this does not mean there are any triangles or any unicorns.

4 Existence is not a predicate or a perfection.

Kant's last point can be summarised as follows:

1 If something adds nothing to the concept of a thing, then it is not part of the essence of the thing.

2 Existence adds nothing to the concept of anything – to say a hundred dollars is real rather than imaginary does not add any characteristics to a dollar.

3 Existence is not part of the essence of a thing; it is not a perfection.

Kant considered that Anselm's argument can be summed up as follows:

1 A perfect being must have all possible perfections,

2 Existence is a possible perfection

3 Therefore any absolutely perfect being must have existence as one of it's perfections.

Kant rejects (2). One can have an idea of something, but however much you develop the idea, you have to go outside it by getting evidence from experience as to whether or not it exists. Kant said:

> The attempt to establish the existence of a supreme being by means of the famous ontological argument of Descartes is ... so much labour and effort lost; we can no more extend our stock of (theoretical) insight by mere ideas, than a merchant can better his

position by adding a few noughts to his cash account. (*Critique of Pure Reason*, Book 11, ch. iii, section 3, ed. Kemp Smith, Macmillan, 1950.)

It was Kant who really put the nail into the coffin of the Ontological Argument. If it is not possible to treat existence as a perfection then there is no way to arrive at the existence of God from a definition of God. However, in recent years a different interpretation has been given to the argument, which has given it new life.

d) What does it mean to say that God exists?

Most of the confusion about the Ontological Argument revolves around a confusion on what it means for God to exist. We have touched on this already in the first section of this book.

Is God's existence more like a bear or a triangle? Is God an object of some sort? If God is an object, then God is rather like a bear – objects are, after all, in time and space. There may or may not be a bear in the road outside (see Martin Lee's article 'Why Is There Something Rather Than Nothing?' – either God is something or nothing). To say God is like a bear is to say God is a 'something', however ineffable. Even if this 'something' is a wholly simple, timeless 'something', then it may or may not exist. Aquinas, Hume, Kant and most traditional believers think that God's existence is like this. God is in some sense an object or substance, a being of some sort, albeit a highly exalted being. If this is so, then Aquinas, Hume and Kant hold we cannot move from the *idea* of God to the reality of God. I may have a perfectly clear idea of a bear but this does not mean there is one.

Hume says that however much our concept of an object may contain, we must go outside it to determine whether or not it exists. We cannot define something into existence, even if it has all the perfections we can imagine.

Bertrand Russell argues that when we say 'Cows exist' what we are really saying is that the *concept* of 'cow' is instantiated whereas the concept of *unicorn* is not. In this, Russell follows Frege who argues that 'exists' tells us that a particular thing is instantiated or exists rather than being a predicate – to say that something exists is to say that the collection of features indicated by the predicate expression of that thing is realised or instantiated. Frege's famous example is

> Tame tigers exist

'Exist' here is not a predicate, it adds nothing to our knowledge of tigers. All it is saying is that there are things which fit our concept of 'tame tigers'. By contrast,

> Tame tigers eat meat

does tell us something about tame tigers – 'eat meat' does, therefore, function as a predicate or a describing word which amplifies what we already know about tame tigers. Russell's point is that however much we define something, however many predicates it may have, we have to have evidence as to whether it exists. This is why all the other arguments for the existence of God start from some features in the world of experience and attempt to establish from these that God exists.

If God is in some sense an 'object', a something, even if a timeless and spaceless substance, then Aquinas is right: the Ontological Argument gets us nowhere. Aquinas did not think that God was an object in any sense like the way we normally use the term: God is not in space or time. Nevertheless, the word 'God' refers successfully to the God who exists beyond space and time and on whom the whole of the created order depends. This God may or may not exist, but we cannot prove God's existence from analysing his nature, which is largely unknowable.

St Anselm's second argument
Anselm has two arguments. The one above occurs in *Proslogion* ch. 2, but the more interesting one may be in *Proslogion*, ch. 3:

And certainly this being so truly exists that it cannot be even thought not to exist. For something can be thought to exist that cannot be thought not to exist, and this is greater than that which can be thought not to exist. Hence, if that-than-which-a-greater-cannot-be-thought can be thought not to exist, then that-than-which-a-greater-cannot-be-thought is not the same as that-than-which-a-greater-cannot-be-thought, which is absurd. Something-than-which-a-greater-cannot-be-thought exists so truly then, that it cannot be even thought not to exist.

And you, Lord our God, are this being. You exist so truly, Lord my God, that you cannot be thought not to exist. And this is as it should be, for if some intelligence could think of something better than You, the creature would be above its creator and would judge its creator – and this is completely absurd. In fact, everything else there is, except You alone, can be thought of as not existing. You alone, then, of all things most truly exist and therefore of all things possess existence to the highest degree; for anything else does not exist as truly, and so possesses existence to a lesser degree. Why then did 'the Fool say in his heart, there is no God' when it is so evident to any rational mind that You of all things exist to the highest degree? Why indeed, unless because he was stupid and a fool?'

Norman Malcolm accepts that the first argument fails. Malcolm begins by stating that if God does not already exist, God cannot come into existence since this would require a cause and would make God a limited being which, by definition, God is not. Similarly, if God already exists, God cannot cease to exist.

Therefore, maintains Malcolm, either God's existence is impossible or it is necessary. Malcolm then argues that God's existence could only be impossible if it were logically absurd or contradictory and, as it is neither, then God's existence *must* be necessary. *The statement 'God necessarily exists,' therefore, can be held to be true.*

Hick rejects this when he maintains that the most that can be said is that if God exists, God exists necessarily. This is problem free *but* there is no way of getting rid of the 'if'. Plantinga maintains that all

Malcolm has shown is that the greatest possible being exists in some possible world, but not necessarily in the real world. To overcome this difficulty, Plantinga differentiates between *maximal excellence* (which entails omnipotence, omniscience and moral perfection) and *maximal greatness* (which entails the property 'has maximal excellence in every possible world'). Plantinga wants to maintain that if God has maximal greatness then God must exist in every possible world. However, Plantinga himself points out the weakness in his own position – one could have another term, *no–maximality* which is the property in a world of having no maximally great being. If this is exemplified in one possible world, it could be exemplified in every possible world.

However, it may be that many people misunderstand what Malcolm is doing. They all assume that he is trying to establish the *de re* necessary God of Aquinas, etc., and this may not be the case.

- Perhaps God is not like this at all.
- Perhaps it means something entirely different to say that God exists,
- Perhaps God should not be considered to be an object in any way at all.

Some people say there is a God and others say there is not. This seems to involve a dispute about a kind of object, a 'something'. However, this may well be an error. Let us remind ourselves of what Anselm says:

> the fool hath said in his heart 'There is no God', but at any rate this very fool, when he hears of this Being of which I speak – a being than which no greater can be conceived – understands what he hears, and what he understands is in his understanding; although he does not understand it to exist. (*Proslogion* in St Anselm's *Basic Writings*, 2nd edition translated by S. N. Deane, Open Court, 1974, chs. 2–4.)

Believers do not go round saying 'God exists', rather, they take part in worship, they pray, go to church, sing hymns and read their Bibles. All these activities *presume* the existence of God. They do not first set out to prove the existence of God and only then go to church. They are either brought up in a group of people who go to church or they come to see the value of belonging to a religious community.

D. Z. Phillips and Fr. Gareth Moore OP (see p. 59ff.), amongst others, consider that to talk of God's existence cannot be considered to be talk about the existence of an object. God is not a something. God is not a substance, rather talk of God is presupposed in the religious way of life. Norman Malcolm sees Anselm's argument as having the force of a grammatical observation. When believers talk of God they are talking of God's inescapable reality to them. It is worth remembering the context in which Anselm put forward his proof. He says in the Preface to his *Proslogion*: 'I have written the following treatise in the person of one who ... seeks to understand what he believes ...'

For Anselm, God's reality is inescapable and he is trying to express this in his argument. He is trying to understand more fully what he already believes. This is very different from trying to prove God's existence to someone who does not accept it. Phillips maintains that the believer is the person for whom God's reality is inescapable. For him or her God could not fail to exist. 'Of course,' he or she might say, 'God exists. God's existence is that on which my whole life is based.'

A parallel might be with the equator (Gareth Moore's example). Of course the equator exists, it is real and exists once one has understood what the equator is. This does not mean, however, that there is a physical line which the equator represents. Instead, the equator is an idea we, in our culture, all accept. We live in a form of life in which the equator is real. The same may be said of God. Within the culture or form of life of the religious believer God is real and exists; God's reality is undoubted. All praise, all exultation, all of the believer's life is related to the reality of God which it does not make sense to doubt. God is the reality to which all of the believer's life is directed. This does not, however, mean that God is an object; rather,

God is a reality within the believer's form of life.

Within this community God is real and exists – but those outside this community do not have any use for language about God. On this basis, the 'fool who has said in his heart there is no God' may be the person who has no use for praise, for worship or for ritual. To him or her, God-talk has no reality.

On this basis, the Ontological Argument may be valuable in pointing us to the sort of reality God has. God is not, on this view, an object. God is not a thing. God is rather an idea within the form of life of the believing community. To the believer, God necessarily exists – like prime numbers exist for the mathematician. It simply does not make sense to deny the reality of God – but this does not mean that God or prime numbers are to be thought of like objects.

Summary

Does the Ontological Argument succeed? It all depends.

If the Ontological Argument seeks to prove that God exists as the creator and sustainer of the universe, whether as timeless substance or as an everlasting Spirit, then it fails for the reasons given by Aquinas, Hume and Kant.

If the Ontological Argument seeks to prove that, in the anti-realist revisionary view of God, God necessarily exists for the believer once the believer has come to understand what the word 'God' means, then the argument has considerable force. Once the believer understands what it means to talk of God, then God exists for him or her. God is a reality within the form of life of religious believers. The fool can only say in his heart that there is no God because he or she has not understood what it means to talk of God. Once he or she does understand what this talk means, he or she will see that God necessarily exists, as talk about God has meaning and value for him or her. The truth of the statement 'God exists' does *not* depend on its correspondence to a Being or Spirit called God, but is rather based on the role the statement plays in the religious person's way of looking at and living in the world. If this is the case, then the

Ontological Argument does succeed in establishing the inescapable reality of God to those who believe.

Questions for consideration

a) What does it mean to say that God necessarily exists?
b) What are the problems with saying that one can arrive at the existence of God by analysing God's nature?
c) What are Aquinas' main reasons for rejecting the Ontological Argument?
d) Give an example of a statement that is analytically true, and another of one that is synthetically true. Describe how you would check whether both these statements are true or not.
e) 'Existence is not a predicate.' What does this mean?
f) Does the Ontological Argument succeed?

NINE

The Design Argument

The heavens declare the glory of God and the firmament showeth his handiwork (Ps. 19. 1).

Design arguments seek to move from facts about the world to God. Early forms of the argument were put forward by Socrates and Plato (see the *Phaedo*). There are various types of argument and different philosophers give them different names. Swinburne (*The Existence of God*) suggests three groups:

- *Teleological Arguments* – Arguments from a general pattern of order in the Universe
- *Arguments from Providence* – Arguments from the provision for the needs; of conscious beings, and
- *The Argument from Beauty*

A distinction may also be drawn between arguments *from* design and arguments *to* design or purpose. The former is close to the Teleological approach and the latter to the Arguments from Providence. It is important to draw a distinction between these two.

Teleological Arguments

Paley's Watchmaker argument is the most famous version. It is an argument based on *analogy* between a watch and the world. The watch shows that it has been made for an intelligent purpose: if we came across a watch, even if we did not know what it was for, it shows all the marks of contrivance and design. Just as the existence of a watch implies a watchmaker, so the existence of the world implies an even greater designer – God. Notice that we do not need to know the purpose of the watch or the universe in order to infer a designer, simply that the design implies a designer.

In the mid-nineteenth century, the interpretation of creation given by Genesis was the first area to be hit by Darwin's work, particularly the idea that God created all animal species with their own nature (Aquinas' position derived from Aristotle) or the Genesis account of a sudden, individual creation of each species in its present form directly by God.

Bishop Samuel Wilberforce at a meeting of the British Association in 1860 said that 'The principle of natural selection ... is absolutely incompatible with the word of God.'

Darwin's theory obviously rejected literal interpretations of the Bible, but it was earlier criticisms that were philosophically more devastating. David Hume (1711–76) effectively rejected Paley's argument 22 years *before* Paley put it forward! It was an indication of the gap between philosophy and theology that Paley (1743–1805) was not aware of Hume's earlier work.

David Hume's *Dialogues concerning Natural Religion* is one of the greatest works on the philosophy of religion ever written. Hume employs three characters:

- CLEANTHES, who believes in Natural Theology and argues a posteriori to God;
- DEMEA, who also believes in God but whose arguments are a priori; and
- PHILO, who is their critic and who puts forward Hume's own views.
  Philo (Hume) has two arguments.

Hume's first argument

Cleanthes first puts forward a version of the Teleological Argument:

1 All design necessarily implies a designer;
2 A great design necessarily implies greatness in the designer;
3 There is clearly great design in the world which is like a great
   machine; therefore,
4 There must be a great designer of the world.

This is very similar to Paley's approach. Central to Cleanthes' whole
approach is that like effects have like causes – he explicitly recognises
that his argument is based on analogy. Hume's criticisms aim
to destroy the argument of Cleanthes by mockery. If like effects
produce like causes, then the logic is that God must be rather like
a superhuman figure – God would be very anthropomorphic.
Possibly there are many Gods, possibly they are male and female,
possibly they are born and die, possibly they are imperfect. Hume
is not denying the design argument works – at least not explicitly.
What he is saying is that if it works it comes up with a limited,
anthropomorphic and imperfect God and his conclusion clearly is
that the design argument is a total failure. He puts his point clearly:

> The world, for aught the user of the design argument knows is
> very faulty and imperfect, compared to a superior standard and
> was only the first rude effort of some infant Deity, who afterwards
> abandoned it, ashamed of his lame performance; it is the work of
> some dependent, inferior Deity; and is the object of derision to
> his superiors; it is the production of old age and dotage in some
> supernatural Deity, and ever since his death, has run on at adven-
> tures, from the first impulse and active force, which it received
> from him ...' (*Dialogues Concerning Natural Religion*, Hackett,
> 1980, Part 5, p. 37).

If we look at the imperfections in the world, particularly the extent
to which nature is 'red in tooth and claw' and the incidence of

natural disasters, earthquakes, tidal waves, disease and the like, this surely points, Hume claims, to malevolence or inadequacy on the part of God. If we saw a badly designed house we would have grave reservations about the architect – the same applies to the world and therefore to God. Hume also argued that if many carpenters collaborate together to build a ship, why should there not be many Gods?

Even if these problems could be overcome, Hume considers, we would still have to question the long and protracted time God took to bring his supposed purposes about. As he puts it:

> Look around this universe. What an immense profusion of beings ... You admire this prodigious variety and fecundity. But inspect a little more narrowly these living creatures ... How hostile and destructive to each other! How insufficient all of them for their own happiness! ... The whole presents nothing but the idea of a blind nature, impregnated by a great vivifying principle, and pouring forth from her lap, without discernment or parental care, her maimed and abortive children. (ibid., p. 74.)

Philo sums up Hume's view by saying:

> All religious systems are subject to great and insuperable difficulties. Each system exposes the absurdities, barbarities and pernicious tenets of its antagonist yet says it is right. All of them on the whole, prepare a complete triumph for the sceptic – a total suspension of judgement is our only reasonable recourse. (ibid., p. 53)

Hume's second argument

Philo's first argument against Cleanthes is that like effects imply like causes, so we end up with a caricature of God. However, he also has a second argument: that it is possible that the universe arose by chance. Philo's second argument accepts that the world is orderly – it behaves in an incredibly orderly manner. Natural laws operate consistently and we can discover them and work with them. Few would deny the order in the universe, but does order imply design? If it does, then design does indeed imply a designer, but the crucial issue is whether the step can be made from order to design.

Philo's second argument can be summarised as follows:

1 The world is ordered.
2 This order either resulted from Design *or* from Chance.
3 It is entirely plausible that the world arose from chance:

   i)   Matter and energy may well be everlasting. We know now, from Einstein, that the stock of matter and energy is constant – matter and energy are continually changing, but the total stock may remain the same.

   ii) If matter and energy are everlasting, then in an infinite number of combinations, every one will be realised (Aquinas implied this in his Third Way)

   iii) Once order has occurred, it will tend to perpetuate itself.

Philo strengthens his argument by another point:

4 Animal adaptation cannot be used to prove a designer of animals since if they did not adapt to their environment they would not survive. It is not legitimate to use what could not be otherwise as evidence of intelligent planning. Philo does admit, however, that it is difficult to explain extra organs not needed for survival such as two eyes or two ears.

Darwin's theories could be used to strengthen Philo's argument here as the theory of natural selection now provides a mechanism which would explain two eyes and two ears as being better suited for survival than one – they increase the field of hearing and of vision and also provide perspective.

Darwin (1809–82) considers that natural selection explains variation. As he puts it:

not only are the various domestic races, but the most distinct genera and orders within the same great class – for instance mammals, birds, reptiles and fishes – are all the descendants of one common progenitor and we must admit that the whole vast amount of difference between these forms has primarily arisen simply from variability ('Variation of Animals and Plants under Domestication', *The Origin of Species by Natural Selection*, ch.).

Philo's judgement is that we should suspend judgement on the question of whether there is a God – there is no firm evidence for or against.

Swinburne has tackled Philo's fourth point:

Suppose that a madman kidnaps a victim and shuts him in a room with a card-shuffling machine. The machine shuffles ten packs of cards simultaneously and then draws a card from each pack and exhibits all the ten cards. The kidnapper tells the victim that he will set the machine to work and it will show its first draw – unless the draw consists of an ace of hearts from each pack, the machine will automatically set off an explosion which will kill the victim so he will not see the cards the machine drew. The machine starts and to the relief of the victim he sees ten Aces. The victim thinks that this extraordinary fact needs an explanation in terms of the machine having been rigged in some way. The kidnapper now reappears and casts doubt on the suggestion. *'It is hardly surprising'* he says *'that the machine draws only aces of hearts. You could not possibly see anything else for you would not be here to see anything at all if any other card had been drawn.'* But, Swinburne says, the victim is right and the kidnapper wrong. There *is* something extraordinary about ten hearts being drawn – the fact that this is a necessary condition of anything being seen is not the point. The Teleologist's basic point that the existence of order is extraordinary is still valid.

Fred Hoyle supports this view:

> A component has evidently been missing from cosmological studies. The origin of the Universe, like the solution of the rubik cube, requires an intelligence (*The Intelligent Universe*, p. 189)

> properties seem to run through the fabric of the natural world like a thread of happy accidents. But there are so many of these odd coincidences essential to life that some explanation seems required to account for them (ibid., p. 220).

Swinburne's conclusion is that the conformity of nature to uniform natural laws is 'too big' a phenomenon for science to explain. Universal orderliness reigns and there are only two possible explanations: Scientific explanation and Personal explanation. Since science cannot explain universal orderliness, the *Personal Explanation*, in terms of God, is the most likely. Be sceptical when Swinburne talks of God as 'personal' – it is important to remember that if God is wholly simple and therefore timeless and spaceless, the meaning given to God's personality is going to be very limited indeed and Swinburne does not recognise this.

In reply to Philo's challenge that we should postulate many gods rather than one since many men co-operate in building a boat, Swinburne argues that this should be rejected. Swinburne admits that Hume acknowledges Ockam's razor:'To multiply causes without necessity is contrary to true philosophy.' However, Hume rejects this principle because if we use the principle of analogy, there is a closer analogy to the idea that many gods co-operate than that there is one God. We have a choice: Hume claims that if we use analogy, it is more probable that there are many gods and that they are rather like human beings. Swinburne claims that the idea of a single God is simpler and has greater explanatory power than many gods and should therefore be preferred.

One of Swinburne's claims is that if there were many deities we would expect to see marks of the handiwork of these deities in different parts of the universe and, by contrast, we see uniformity everywhere which points to one deity (p. 142). This seems to be a weak argument – after all, as Hume says, many people co-operate in the building of a ship yet there is only a single design. It is worth thinking hard about Swinburne's criterion of 'simplicity' – Ockam's razor works in science but whether God can conceivably be regarded as a 'simple' explanation (as opposed to being metaphysically simple which is very complex indeed) is highly debatable.

Swinburne maintains that God is the more probable hypothesis because God would have reason to create a universe with finite creatures who have the chance to grow to knowledge of God and an orderly universe from which human beings can learn. So Swinburne concludes (p. 147):

1 A priori it is very improbable that a universe could just happen to exist; and
2 By virtue of God's postulated character, this is the sort of universe God would have good reason to make.

Swinburne therefore maintains that whilst the Teleological Argument by itself does not make it probable that God exists, the argument does serve to increase the probability of God's existence.

This success of the Teleological Argument depends on being able to arrive at the existence of God and some ideas about what God is like from the design or order in the world and it may be difficult to see how Swinburne has refuted Hume's arguments. The argument depends on there being close analogies between the creator of something within the world and the creation of the world as a whole. The more dissimilarities are argued between human construction and the world (in order to reject Hume's anthropomorphic approach), the weaker the argument by analogy becomes. The stronger the analogies, the stronger the anthropomorphic view of God that emerges. It may be argued that the creator of a steam train does not have to look like a steam train and, therefore, that there are not close parallels between the creator and creation. However, Hume's challenge is that the more we want to make the design argument succeed, the more the creator of the universe must be like the creator of steam trains and other things in the universe – and this would be too anthropomorphic a picture of God.

Richard Dawkins in *The Blind Watchmaker* follows Hume and describes approaches like Swinburne's as 'Arguments from personal incredulity'. He effectively says that the fact that a Professor of the Philosophy of Religion sitting in his study at Oxford, who has never studied biology, and who cannot off the top of his head think of a reason for polar bears, does not entitle him to say that God is the best explanation. Dawkins' view is that the hypothesis of God is entirely superflous and that order is due to natural selection alone – 'a blind, unconscious, automatic process' which is completely without purpose, hence the title of his book:

> Evolution has no long term goal. There is no long distance target, no final perfection to serve as a criterion for selection ... The criteria for selection are always short term, either simply survival or, more generally, reproductive success ... The 'watchmaker' that is cumulative natural selection is blind to the future and has no long term goal (p. 58).

Richard Dawkins has popularised the evolutionary and sociological principle of 'The Selfish Gene' (in his book by that name). According to this theory, people do not do things for the good of their community or friends or even themselves, but simply in order to enable human genes to survive. As Dawkins puts it: 'We are survival machines – robot vehicles blindly programmed to preserve the selfish molecules known as genes.' Some biologists such as Stephen Rose, Richard Lewontin and Jay Gould reject Dawkins' view: they maintain that whole organisms and species have a clear priority over our genes. However, in a book published at the end of 1996, Matt Ridley (*The Origins of Virtue*) considers that Dawkins' opponents have misunderstood the idea of the Selfish Gene and he attempts to make the position clearer. Ridley maintains that whilst human genes are undoubtedly selfish, humans have developed so that we have the ability to override our nature and to act virtuously. Effectively Ridley is saying that although we are, in essence, depraved due to our essential biological and genetic nature, we have evolved to the point where we can overcome this nature. Ridley says: 'The first thing we should do to create a good society ... is to conceal the truth about humankind's propensity for self-interest, the better to delude our fellows into thinking that they are noble savages inside.'

John Cornwall, in a review of Ridley's book in *The Sunday Times* of November 3, 1996, says that, for Ridley

> Selfishness is underpinned by science at the level of the molecules; whilst virtue is founded on make-believe ... But Ridley overlooks the strength of the central Judeo–Christian paradox; that each individual is simulaneously fallen and exalted, each individual capable of vice and yet authentically endowed with dignity.

Certainly the idea of humans being fundamentally evil yet being able to overcome this could fit well into traditional Christianity.

There have been replies to Dawkins, not least from Arthur Peacocke (a physical biologist and a theologian writing in *Science and the Theology of Creation*). He claims that even if a complete explanation, a unified theory, could be found, this does not rule out God. There is still a need to explain 'how our universe came into being ...' and 'why there is only one set of physical laws ...'. God is still possible as some sort of ground of being.

John Polkinghorne maintains that God chose to create a universe governed by chance and law:

> The universe that we actually perceive with its balanced and fruitful interplay of chance and necessity, novelty and regularity, is a world that one might expect as the work of a creator both loving and faithful, for it incorporates the two gifts of freedom and relia-

bility. (*One World – the Interaction of Science and Theology*, SPCK, 1986, p. 92.)

The difference between believer and non-believer over the design arguments depends, to some degree, on the issue raised in the Cosmological Argument, namely What is the fundamental explanation for the universe? If the universe itself, with its laws and regularities, is the fundamental explanation, then the hypothesis of God is not required. If, however, some explanation is required for the universe, then God provides such an explanation.

Even if the Teleological Argument succeeds, there are real questions as to the sort of God one arrives at. John Stuart Mill (*Three Essays on Religion*) raised this problem: maintaining that given the apparent imperfections in the universe and the amount of natural evils that occur, the most plausible hypothesis was either to deny the Designer's goodness *or* to deny the Designer's omnipotence. Mill chose to maintain God's goodness and hence concluded that God must be limited – what or by whom he could not tell. Mill's book, like that of Hume, is very well worth reading. Mill is willing to accept there is a designer, but it is the attributes of the Designer he challenges. An imperfect universe implies limitation of the designer and hence Mill arrives at a limited God.

If design in the world is to be used as an argument for God's existence, then evil, animal suffering and disease all need to be explained in any account of the Designer. The issue is whether the world, as we know it, really is such as to point to an all-powerful and wholly good creator. Does not evil and suffering either show lack of purpose or, at least, a God who is limited? It is important to recognise that there is a difference between (a) The Design Argument, which asks whether one can arrive at God, and if so what sort of God, from the facts in the universe, and (b) The Problem of Evil, which asks whether, given belief in an all-powerful and wholly good God, this belief can be reconciled with the evil in the world. This latter issue is dealt with in *The Puzzle of Evil* (Peter Vardy, HarperCollins, 1992).

What may be regarded as extraordinary and in need of explanation is the drive for complexity inherent in the evolutionary process. If survival alone is the sole criterion for success, then it would seem reasonable to assume that single-cell organisms could survive very effectively, yet the whole of evolution seems to be driven towards greater and greater complexity resulting in the emergence of intelligence of a very high order and based on great complexity. There seems no clear reason why this should be so and the idea of an intelligence driving evolution might be held to be plausible.

At most, the Teleological Argument may show that there is some intelligence responsible for the universe, but what form this intelligence takes and whether it can be identified with the Christian God the argument may not be able to demonstrate.

The Argument from Providence

The Teleological Argument is derived from the general pattern of order in the universe. The argument from Providence, by contrast, is an argument for the provision for the needs of intelligent beings within the universe. Notice that these two arguments are distinct: sometimes they are separated by referring to the Argument *from* and the Argument *to* Design.

A. E. Taylor put forward the classical form of the Argument from Providence, although Swinburne also has such an argument. Taylor's approach is as follows:

1 Nature seems to plan in advance for the needs of animals and humans. This planning cannot be accounted for by physical laws alone since there are innumerable ways that electrons could run. There must be more than physical laws to account for the tremendously high improbability of life.

2 Mind or intelligence is needed to explain how this improbable state of affairs could be brought about. Human beings plan ahead and nature gives evidence of similar planning.

3 Mind cannot be explained by evolution, since evolution itself requires a Mind which imposed it.

4 Human beings cannot be explained simply by evolution, since humans do not just adapt to the environment, they transform it.

Taylor's argument is an attempt to restore the Teleological Argument, taking Darwin into account. But Darwin can still be convincing – even the ability to transform our environment is a feature that enables humankind to survive more effectively. It is true that the source of the basic mechanism of natural selection is not explained by Darwin, but we are then back to the ultimate problem: Which is more probable, God or the brute fact of the universe? Believers will opt for God and non-believers will opt for the claim that the universe 'just is'. Much will depend on personal opinion.

Taylor ends by postulating God as 'Mind' – note the similarity to Swinburne's 'Personal explanation' – but, again, there is an issue as to what it might mean to say that God has 'mind' if God is wholly simple. Certainly timeless, spaceless God does not have a mind, and to apply such language to God can only be done analogically and with very limited content indeed.

The following quote from Darwin may be of interest: 'What a book a Devil's chaplain might write on the clumsy, wasteful, blundering, law and horribly cruel works of nature.' It can be worth considering how one might reply to the 'Devil's chaplain'.

Darwin's evolutionary approach, although widely accepted, has not yet been proved. It is important to be careful not to accept as 'obvious' something that may not be. Wittgenstein put this well:

One circle of admirers [of Darwin] say 'Of course' whilst others said 'Of course not!' ... Why in the hell should anyone say 'Of Course'? ... Did anyone see this process happening? No. Has anyone seen it happening now? No. The evidence of breeding is just a drop in the bucket. But there were thousands of books in which this was said to be the obvious solution. People were certain on grounds which were extremely thin (*Lectures and Conversations on Aesthetics, Psychology and Religious Belief,* Blackwell, 1966, p. 26).

This is not, of course, to say that Darwin was mistaken, but simply to make the point that it is easy to regard something as certain that is later shown to be false. Fashion can play a key role on those things about which we consider doubt to be impossible and what is 'undoubted' at one point may be held to be 'certainly mistaken' at another. The flat-earth theory is a case in point and the history of science is a history of theories once considered irrefutable being refuted.

Admittedly the beginning of life and the drive to complexity in organisms once life has been formed have not been explained by current theories. There is no evidence that life could arise spontaneously, indeed, the evidence that it could so arise is very thin indeed. Even granted the billions of suns and the billions of years of the universe's existence, the beginnings of life seem very improbable. Once life has begun, then evolution would seem to imply that any basic form of life should simply perpetuate itself and there seems to be no reason why there should be a drive for greater and greater complexity and for the emergence of intelligence. It may be that there are scientific explanations for both these steps that have not been discovered but these gaps in the explanation (and they are very important gaps) could leave room for believers to affirm a role for a creator God to 'breathe fire into the equations'. Such a God, it might be held, is needed to direct matter and the laws that govern matter towards the evolution of higher intelligences such as human beings.

The Argument from Beauty

Beauty is held to have no survival value nor has human appreciation of beauty any apparent real value in helping humans to live together or to be more effectively in the environment within which they find themselves. Naturally there is a survival value in females and males finding each other attractive, but what is the survival advantage in seeing the beauty in a snowflake; the beauty of a spring morning or a piece of music? The ability to appreciate beauty, therefore, may be held to be a pointer towards God implanted in human beings to make them indirectly aware of God's presence.

F. R. Tennant (*Philosophical Theology*, Vol. 2, Cambridge University Press, 1930, pp. 89–93) put forward this argument maintaining that the universe is not just beautiful in places – it is saturated with beauty from the microscopic to the macroscopic level. There is no particular reason to expect a beautiful rather than an ugly world and perhaps the presence of beauty and human appreciation of it may be seen as signs that God wishes to draw us towards the Divine rather than to be simply content with survival.

The Franciscan tradition in particular, stemming from St Francis of Assisi and St Bonaventure, maintains that God is beautiful and the beauty of the world attracts us to God. A modern Franciscan theologian, Paul Rout, puts it as follows:

Sometimes beauty overwhelms us, such as when we are struck by the beauty of the natural world in the overpowering majesty of a sunset, for example. In apprehending something as beautiful, we come to find it desirable. We are not involved in an intellectual exercise; it is more that we are drawn beyond ourselves and our rational concepts by what is desirable. The language of such experience can help us speak about God whose goodness and beauty overwhelms us and captivates the one who seeks with an open and listening heart. It is language which can offer hope and meaning to those many who are grown disillusioned with the sterile world of clinical efficiency and are yearning for the eruption of the beautiful (Paul Rout, *Francis and Bonaventure*, Fount Christian Thinkers series, Fount, 1996, p. 73).

As an argument, this would be unlikely to convince the sceptic, but nevertheless many have found the beauty of the universe a real pointer to the existence of an intelligence behind it.

One problem is whether human apprehension of beauty is a matter of cultural conditioning – in other words, is beauty 'present' in the universe independently of one being aware of it or is it only that human beings see things as beautiful. To put it another way, are you a realist about beauty?

Summary

1 If the Design Argument is to be taken seriously it must recognise the facts about the world from which it is working. These facts apparently include natural selection; the presence of great beauty; the higher human capacities, such as love, unselfishness and morality; the pain and suffering human beings cause one another; the suffering of animals and suffering due to natural disasters beyond human control.

2 If the argument is to succeed, these facts must point to a God who, if the traditional Christian, Jewish or Muslim God, must be *omnipotent* (all-powerful), *omniscient* (all-knowing) and *wholly good*. We shall define these terms with greater precision later in this book. Some modern theologians have supported the idea of a limited and suffering God, and this approach might well be supported by the Design Argument as it might be held that any God who created the universe with its apparent defects must be limited by factors of which we have no knowledge. For the moment, the reader must decide whether the facts we know about the world make the existence of such a God more probable or not.

3 The argument rests on probability and individual judgement. It is not, therefore, going to be conclusive, and much will depend on each individual's reaction to it. Philosophically this sort of value judgement is not easy to justify, and the argument may owe more to its persuasive power than to its logic.

There are no final answers to be found in philosophy although philosophy and science are beginning to share mutual concerns and are perplexed by similar problems. Paul Davies puts it like this:

The central theme ... is that, through science, we human beings are able to grasp at least some of nature's secrets. We have cracked part of the cosmic code. Why this should be, just why Homo Sapiens should carry the spark of rationality that provides the key to the universe, is a deep enigma. We, who are children of the universe – animated stardust – can nevertheless reflect on the nature of that same universe, even to the extent of glimpsing the rules on which it runs. How we have become linked into this cosmic dimension is a mystery. Yet the linkage cannot be denied(*The Mind of God*, p. 232).

Science and Theology both end in unexplained mysteries and both, at their best, should be willing to pursue an open-minded search into the unknown.

Questions for consideration

a) What is the argument from Providence?
b) Does Darwin's theory of evolution totally undermine the Design argument?
c) 'The beauty of the world points to the existence of a creator God.' Is this claim justified?
d) 'If the world has a designer, this designer must be limited.' Do you agree?
e) Do you agree that human beings can be entirely explained in evolutionary terms?
f) Are science and religion opposed?

TEN

The Argument from Religious Experience

It was late that Sunday evening and the disciples were gathered together behind locked doors, because they were afraid of the Jewish authorities. Then Jesus came and stood among them. 'Peace be with you,' he said. After saying this he showed them his hands and his side ... One of the twelve disciples, Thomas (called the twin), was not with them when Jesus came. So the other disciples told him, 'We have seen the Lord.' Thomas said to them, 'Unless I see the scars of the nails in his hands and put my finger in those scars and my hand in his side, I will not believe' (John 20:19–24).

Imagine you were walking along the banks of Loch Ness. Suddenly there was a tremendous commotion in the water and a green head appeared with loops behind it. The weather was good and the head and its loops swam nearer shore. You could see it clearly as well as the markings and the scales – you could see that it did not appear to be a model or manmade. You had not been drinking nor had you been taking drugs. To you, the Loch Ness monster would be real and no matter how much evidence there was against its existence, you might well believe in its existence.

To those who do not believe in religion, claims to religious experience are as incredulous as claims to have seen the Loch Ness monster or to have seen UFOs – yet many people stake their lives on such experiences. The first question to be asked is whether it is possible to argue from such experiences to the existence of God. On the face of it this seems plausible – we normally rely on our senses and empiricists hold that our senses provide us with the foundation for all our claims to knowledge.

What is religious experience?

It is very easy to waffle on about religious experience without defining what it is! There are many different ways of categorising such experience and Swinburne's provides one such analysis (set out in *The Existence of God*, Oxford University Press, 1979). The main difference he draws is between *public* and *private* religious experiences and he then divides these further.

Public experiences

1 An individual sees God or God's action in a public object or scene. However, the purported religious experience can readily be explained on other grounds. For instance, the believer might look at the night sky and see the hand of God, whilst the non-believer might just see a beautiful sunset. In this case a great deal depends on personal interpretations.

2 Very unusual public events occur, involving a breach of natural law. Examples might include someone walking on water or a person appearing in a locked room or water turning into wine. There is less emphasis on personal interpretation here, although the sceptic can still maintain that whilst something inexplicable may have occurred, there is no need to attribute this to God. A hundred years ago a video camera might have been considered miraculous, whereas today it is simply an example of modern technology.

Private experiences

By their very nature, these are less easily verified than public experiences:

1 Experiences which an individual can describe using normal language. Examples might include Jacob's vision of a ladder going up

to heaven or the appearance of the Angel Gabriel to Mary. There is, of course, always a problem with the interpretation of dreams, and many would look for psychological rather than divine explanations of them.

2 Experiences which cannot be described in normal language but which are nevertheless very real to those experiencing them. Mystical experiences are the most obvious examples of this category. The mystic may be the first to admit that normal language is not adequate to express what has happened. These experiences may be of great intensity and may be of various types. Often the mystic will resort to contradictions in order to try to express himself. For example: 'Black did not cease to be black, nor white cease to be white, but black became white and white became black.'

3 In this case, there is no specific experience, but the individual feels that God is acting in his or her life. Looking back on past events, the individual may say, 'God's hand guided me,' although if pressed he or she would admit that there is no specific evidence for this.

There is a substantial difference between, say, seeing the night sky as God's handiwork or seeing the sun come to a standstill in the sky and a vague, interior feeling of the presence of 'The Holy'. The fourth of the above categories is a mystical experience which it is hard to describe in normal language – the following quotation from *The Wind in the Willows* is an excellent description of such an experience:

Breathless and transfixed, the Mole stopped rowing as the liquid run of that glad piping broke in on him like a wave, caught him up, and possessed him utterly. He saw the tears on his comrade's cheeks, and bowed his head and understood ... 'This is the place of my song-dream, the place the music played to me,' whispered the Rat, as if in a trance. 'Here, in this holy place, here if anywhere, surely we shall find Him!' Then suddenly the Mole felt a great Awe fall upon him, an awe that turned his muscles to water, bowed his head, and rooted his feet to the ground. It was no panic terror – indeed he felt wonderfully at peace and happy – but it was an awe that smote and held him and, without seeking, he knew it could only mean that some August Presence was very, very near. With difficulty he turned to look at his friend, and saw him at his side cowed, stricken, and trembling violently. And still there was utter silence in the populous bird-haunted branches around them; and still the light grew and grew ...

'Rat!' he found breath to whisper, shaking. 'Are you afraid?'

'Afraid?' murmured the Rat, his eyes shining with unutterable love. 'Afraid of HIM? O, never, never! And yet –and yet – O, Mole, I am afraid!'

Then the two animals, crouching to the earth, bowed their heads and did worship.

Caroline Franks Davies describes religious experience as

something akin to a sensory experience

an intellectual intuition which is analagous to our intuition of other human persons in so far as firstly, it is mediated by signs and secondly, it terminates in spiritual reality

a roughly datable mental event which the subject is to some extent aware of

experiences which the subjects themselves describe in religious terms or which are intrinsically religious (quotes from Davies' *The Evidential Force of Religious Experience*, Oxford University Press, 1989, pp. 31–2).

Martin Buber talks of an encounter with God as an 'I/Thou' encounter. In other words, God is encountered not as some abstract principle or as some prime mover, but as a 'Thou' – an essentially personal reality. Believers may claim that their encounter with God is so real and so immediate that no justification is required. John Hick likens this to a man being asked to justify being in the presence of his wife and maintains that no such justification is required. Nevertheless the possibility of being mistaken is real as the evidence in favour of being in the presence of one's wife may be held to be higher than the evidence for being in the presence of God.

John Wisdom's famous *gardener* example illustrates this. Two people look at a neglected garden. One is convinced a gardener is there because of the signs of order and beauty there. The other denies this and points to the weeds and the signs of disorder. They devise various tests but no sign of a gardener is found. The first person, however, sticks to his belief and maintains that there *is* a gardener, but it is an incorporeal, invisible gardener. The two people do not differ about the facts of the garden – their difference arises due to their different interpretations. The problem, of course, is to know which of the two people are 'right', if, indeed, there is any right answer.

A. E. Taylor maintains that the person with the artist's eye sees beauty everywhere and similarly the religious person sees everything in terms of the reality of God. Taylor is effectively maintaining that it is the believer who sees things correctly, however, no real evidence is given. The artist may have learnt to see beauty in every situation, no matter how apparently grim and hideous. Similarly, the religious believer may have been taught to experience the world *as if* it is infused by God.

Religious experiences can be divided into two broad types:

- *External*: e.g. 'I was aware of the presence of Mary near my bed', and
- *Internal*: e.g. 'I had an experience of it seeming to me that Mary was by my bed.'

One immediate problem is how one moves from the second of these to the first. 'Seems' in the second case implies that the person concerned trusts that the experience is reliable but accepts the possibility of being in error. The problem is obvious: how does one move from the *conviction* that a person has experienced God to the claim that he or she actually *did* experience God?

Bridging the Internal/External gap

Swinburne has attempted to address the issue of how one moves from the claim of interior certainty about a religious experience to the claim that this experience is an independent reality. He puts forward a Cumulative Argument for the existence of God. The first step in this approach is to look at all the various arguments for God's existence *except* the argument from Religious Experience. Swinburne believes that none of these arguments, by themselves, succeed in proving that God exists but, put together, they do succeed in showing that God's existence is a reasonable possibility. *Given this*, he then proceeds to put forward his argument from Religious Experience. This latter argument rests on two important principles as part of a Cumulative Argument for the existence of God:

1 *The Principle of Credulity* maintains that it is a principle of rationality that (in the absence of special considerations) if it seems to a person that X is present, then probably X is present. What one seems to perceive is probably so.

2 *The Principle of Testimony* maintains that, in the absence of special considerations, it is reasonable to believe that the experiences of others are probably as they report them.

Swinburne maintains that if we refuse to accept the first of these principles we land in a sceptical bog. We should, therefore, allow religious experiences initial credibility unless there is some evidence against them (if, for instance, we have been drinking or the light is bad or there is the possibility of some trick being played by the light).

The Puzzle of God

The aim of the Principle of Credulity is to put the onus on the sceptic to show why reports of religious experience should not be accepted. This is important – the principle seeks to establish initial credibility and that claims to religious experience should not be dismissed out of hand. The sceptic should, it is held, produce argument or evidence to show why claims to religious experience should not be accepted as valid. In the absence of such argument or evidence, then, the claims should be taken at face value.

The Principle of Testimony simply relies on the inherent trustworthiness of other people, it asks us to believe reports of experiences unless we have some grounds for not doing so. If, for instance, a person is known to be unreliable, is on drugs, suffers from delusions or otherwise has a previous history which would cast doubt on his or her reliability, then we would be right to be suspicious of what we are told. However, if the person is apparently of sound mind, of reasonable intelligence and is generally reliable, then there is no reason, in principle, why we should not believe them.

Caroline Franks Davies in her excellent book, *The Evidential Force of Religious Experience*, builds on Swinburne's approach. Effectively she and Swinburne work with a cumulative argument. They maintain that if all the arguments for and against the existence of God are considered, they are fairly evenly balanced. Some of the arguments strengthen the likelihood that God exists whilst others (for instance those concentrating on the problem of evil and suffering) make the existence of God less likely. If these are all taken together, then, it is held, it is neither highly probable nor highly improbable that God exists – the scales of probability are evenly balanced. *Given this situation*, it is reasonable to rely on reports of religious experience to tip the scales in favour of belief that God exists.

Neither Swinburne nor Davies give sufficient weight to counter arguments against belief in God. For instance, they give scant attention to the problem of evil and whilst their arguments may be persuasive to an existing believer, to an unbiased observer they would have rather less force. The existence of evil does significantly reduce the probability that the God of Christian theism exists,

118

although how one balances the probability for and against God's existence will inevitably be a largely subjective matter about which opinions will differ.

What is the evidence?

It is not easy collecting evidence about religious experience. Many people do not want to speak about their experiences and often such experiences are not easy to describe. People fear ridicule, being made fun of and mocked and therefore keep quiet. We live in a world in which the whole idea of religious experience is often greeted with great scepticism. If, therefore, one is to proceed rationally one should examine dispassionately and without bias whatever evidence is available. If one starts from the conviction that religious experiences cannot occur or, on the other hand, if one starts by being convinced that religious experiences are common, then it is unlikely that one's mind will be changed.

David Hay in 1986 wrote an important book called *Inner Space*. This brought together research conducted by the Oxford Religious Experience research unit. Essentially between about 25 and 45 per cent of the population of Britain, irrespective of age, geographical position or even belief say that they have been aware of a presence or power beyond themselves. The book records that many of the people interviewed had never previously spoken about their experiences because they thought that others would make fun of them or would not understand. The data was collected by reputable and independent polling organizations. These impressive figures cannot be lightly dismissed. They do not prove the matter, but they must be taken into account by any open-minded enquirer as part of the overall equation. It should be noted, however, that the claims are fairly general and it is difficult to translate them into the faith claims of any one, single religion.

In addition, many great saints have claimed to have been directly aware of the presence of God – people like St Francis of Assisi, St John of the Cross, Julian of Norwich, Ignatius of Loyola, Teresa of

Lisieux and many others have claimed to be directly aware of God's presence. Of course, they could have been deceived, but one has to take their testimony seriously, particularly when their intelligence is evident from their writings.

Challenges against religious experience

Various challenges can be put forward against the whole idea that religious experience is a valid pointer to the existence of God. Caroline Franks Davies lists the following types of challenges:

Description-related challenges

These dismiss claims to experience something when the description is self-contradictory or inconsistent. Such challenges can be defeated by showing that there is no real contradiction or inconsistency, in other words, that the idea of God does not involve any contradiction.

Subject-related challenges

These dismiss experiential claims because the person claiming the experience is unreliable or, for instance, has not had the proper training to correctly evaluate the experience. Davies maintains, however, that in the case of religious experiences a very simple person may have as profound an experience as a more sophisticated one. Further, even much religious training or guidance by a spiritual master does not guarantee that a religious experience will result.

Object-related challenges

If, on the basis of background evidence, it is highly unlikely that the thing claimed to be experienced was present, then the claim might be dismissed. The Loch Ness monster or pink elephants might fall into this category. The point about Swinburne's cumulative case argument is to show that this is not the case with experiences of God.

Other more specific challenges include the following:

a) The vicious circle challenge

Anthony Flew claims that the character of religious experience

> seem[s] to depend on the interests, background and expectations of those who have them rather than on anything separate and autonomous ... the expert natural historian of religious experience would be altogether astonished to hear of the vision of Bernadette occurring not to a Roman Catholic at Lourdes, but to a Hindu at Bewares, or of Apollo manifest not in classical Delphi but in Kyoto under the Shoguns.(*God and Philosophy*, Hutchinson, 1966, p. 126–7.)

Davies rejects this challenge on the grounds that it applies largely to visions. Also, she claims that the person in one tradition will tend to use the language and ideas of the tradition to explain their experiences. However, there is an important assumption being made here, namely that one can strip away the description and arrive at a common core of meaning or a 'raw, pre-conceptual experience'. This seems highly debatable, as experiences and the concepts in which they are expressed are tied together closely and, in any case, how could one claim that an experience of Mary at Lourdes or of Vishnu or Kali were experiences of the same thing unless one has criteria (which can only be given in language) to validate the claim to 'sameness'? In the absence of such criteria, the claim that all religious experiences are really of the same reality seems closer to an assertion than an argued position. There is, in effect, no evidence for the claim without public criteria to support it – and this is generally absent precisely because of the non-specific nature of religious experience.

The conflicting claims challenge

If religious experience does provide evidence for the truth of religion, then for which religion does it provide evidence? Most religions make claims that conflict with each other. The Christian claims that Jesus is the Son of God and God is triune; the Muslim claims God is unitary, that Jesus was simply a prophet who did not die on the cross and that Mohammed is the supreme prophet to whom the Koran was dictated. Jews reject Jesus' divinity and also Mohammed's role. Mainstream Buddhism does not maintain belief in a God in any direct way similar to the monotheistic religions. There is a frequent claim made by Western liberals that all religions are really the same, but the basis for the claim is often scanty. If religious experience justifies one religion, then why should it not justify all? And it may be held to be more probable that it is the individual's *prior beliefs* that shape whatever interior experience they claim to have. Stace even goes so far as to claim that many reported experiences are 'shaped' and determined by pressure from Church authorities.

This is a powerful challenge as if there is a 'common transcendental core' giving rise to mystical and other religious experiences, it is likely to be so vague and general that it will have little in common with the claims about ultimate reality made by any one religion.

The psychological challenge

This maintains that many purported religious experiences can be reduced to psychological states and when an individual claims to have had a religious experience, in fact she is experiencing her ego or superego and there is no external referent. However, it must be recognised that although a psychologist may claim that many religious experiences can be explained in psychological terms, this does not mean that *all* religious experiences can be thus explained – there may be an unexplained residue which could still point to an external referent; and even if the psychological explanation is accepted, the believer can still maintain that God works *through* psychology.

However the second point raises the problem that if one has to rely on one's prior beliefs before accepting religious experiences as valid, this means that such experiences do not justify belief, rather they may operate within belief. They have no epistemological role (which means they do not act as a basis for faith).

Realism and anti-realism related to religious experience

We have already seen that the anti-realist rejects the idea that the word 'God' refers to any being or spirit beyond the 'form of life' which the believer inhabits. Religious experience will be seen as something *internal* to a particular belief system; in other words, instead of religious experience being the basis for faith, the believer will be *taught* to experience the world religiously from an early age and will come to associate particular smells and atmospheres as having something to do with 'The Divine'. Experiences are labelled religious, therefore, as a result of individuals being educated into a framework of beliefs. The night sky will be described by the non-believer as simply being 'beautiful' whilst the believer will see it as 'the hand of God'. This comes back to Wisdom's gardener, although the anti-realist will deny that any realist claim is being made. Instead, all we have is a clash of perceptual frameworks. The difference between realist and anti-realist is vital in understanding different interpretations of religious experience.

Caroline Franks Davies effectively relies on the claim that individuals can experience the divine directly, that it is possible for the individual, in some way or another, to be aware of the divine reality that transcends everything in the created order. The exact content of this 'divine' is by no means clear and certainly such claimed experiences would not support the detailed theological claims made by many of the major world religions. However, the important claim is that there *is* a Divine which can be experienced directly. Christian and Islamic mystics have traditionally made similar claims and at the beginning of our own century the fundamental importance of such experiences was given expression by William James.

William James' book *Varieties of Religious Experience* (Cambridge and Harvard University Presses, 1985) is a classic text in mysticism. It was written early this century and maintains that religious experience is primary and acts as a foundation for faith. James rejects philosophy and sees religion as being founded on something other than reason. Thus he says:

> What seriousness can possibly remain in debating philosophic propositions that will never make an appreciable difference to us in action? ... What is the deduction of [God's] metaphysical attributes but a shuffling and matching of pedantic dictionary adjectives, aloof from morals, aloof from human needs ... verbality has stepped into the place of vision ... What keeps religion going is something other than abstract definitions and systems of concatenated adjectives, and something different from faculties of theology and their professors. (ibid., pp. 342–5)

This leads James to his classic definition of religion as

> the feelings, acts and experiences of individual men in their solitude, so far as they apprehend themselves to stand in relation to whatever they may consider the divine (ibid., p. 34).

Effectively James is maintaining that religious experience is fundamental and creeds as well as statements regarding propositional beliefs are secondary accretions laid on top of the experiences that form the essence of true religion. James sets out four marks of mystical experience (and it is such experiences on which he concentrates):

1 ineffability (mysticism like love needs to be directly experienced in order to be understood);

2 noetic quality (mystics speak of revelations and illuminations which are held to provide knowledge and transcend rational categories);

3 transiency (mystical experiences last for a short time but 'modify the inner life of the subject between the times of their occurrence'); and

4 passivity where the experience is beyond the individual's control and cannot be obtained by effort; it is a gift.

James' understanding of the 'divine' is broad:

> we must interpret the term divine very broadly ... the divine shall mean for us only such a primal reality as the individual feels impelled to respond to solemnly and gravely.

However, James' understanding of how or when religious experience may occur is more narrow:

> the individual transacts ... by himself alone, and the ecclesiastical organisation, with its priests and sacraments and other go-betweens, sinks to an altogether secondary place. The relation goes direct from heart to heart, from soul to soul, between man and his maker.

James, like most writers on spirituality, believes the validity of 'religious experience' must be judged by the fruits unique to this type of experience:

> that element or quality in them which we can meet nowhere else

which he summarises as

> ... Saintliness ... spiritual emotions are the habitual centre of the personal energy; there is a certain composite photograph of universal saintliness, the same in all religions ...

and this, like primary experience, is common to saintly figures in world religions where the four 'fruits' of primary religious experience may be found:

1 A feeling of being in a wider life than that of this world's little interests; and a conviction ... of the existence of an Ideal Power.

2 A sense of the friendly continuity of the ideal power with our own life, and a willing self-surrender to its control.

3 An immense elation and freedom, as the outlines of the confining selfhood melt down.

4 A shifting of the emotional centre towards loving and harmonious affections ... Asceticism ... Strength of the soul ... Purity ... Charity ... Religious rapture, moral enthusiasm, ontological wonder, cosmic emotion, are all unifying states of mind ...

The validity of religious experience can only be judged by its fruits. The person having the experience is compelled to self-surrender, and paradoxically the passivity required results in vital new life. Many false claims are made by people regarding religious experiences when their lives do not reflect it; words are not enough – it has to be felt:

> Whoever not only says, but feels, 'God's will be done,' is mailed against every weakness; ... martyrs, missionaries, and religious reformers [are] there to prove the tranquil-mindedness, under naturally agitating or distressing circumstances, which self-surrender brings.

In genuine religious experiences, James claims, 'God' imparts a new perspective where things that may trouble others now have no power:

> the disappearance of all fear from one's life, the quite indescribable and inexplicable feeling of an inner security, which one can only experience, but which, once it has been experienced, one can never forget.

This can set such people apart as others may not understand:

> it is religion's secret, and to understand it you must yourself have

been a religious man of the extremer type.

To know is to understand. James acknowledges that his definitions of religious experience and the divine are broad:

> we are dealing with a field of experience where there is not a single conception that can be sharply drawn ... Things are more or less divine, states of mind are more or less religious, reactions are more or less total, but the boundaries are always misty, and it is everywhere a question of amount and degree.

James is ambiguous about the nature of the God which is experienced, but the crucial point of his book is that those who have the experiences, experience the divine as something 'other' than their psyche. Whether it *is* something other, is not a point that James seeks to prove or establish.

Professor Nicholas Lash, in *Easter in Ordinary* (University of Notre Dame Press, 1990) produces a fierce attack on William James' whole approach. By implication Lash also rejects the idea that religious experience can serve as a grounding for faith. He rejects James' whole approach root and branch, particularly James' emphasis on the individual and the ability of the individual to apprehend the divine directly.

Lash mocks James' position as seeing religion depending on a minority of 'pattern setters', a small minority who have religious experiences and who others are meant to follow (given the work of the Oxford Religious Experience Research Unit there seem to be many more people who have such experiences than Lash allows). Lash rejects the idea of God as cause of the world: there is 'no event or occurrence in the world for which the best explanation would be "God did it"' (*Easter in Ordinary*, pp. 224–5).

It is noteworthy how very similar this is to Gareth Moore's rejection of the idea of God as a cause in his book *Thinking about God*. Moore agrees with Aquinas in saying that God is not a thing – things are in space and time, they are objects. However, Moore goes much further than Aquinas as Moore holds that God is *nothing*, there is nothing that is God. This seems very similar to Lash's position. Further, Lash says, 'being in relation with God' makes 'no particular difference' (op. cit., p. 250). The reason for this soon becomes clear in Lash's rejection of Karl Rahner. Lash quotes Rahner as saying: 'Creation strictly, as such, contains no absolute mysteries' (op. cit., p. 237).

Rahner's point is to contrast the solvable mysteries of the world with the Holy Mystery that is God. Rahner's thought, Lash maintains (and he quotes George Vass) is 'infected with the Dualistic Cartesianism still lurking at the back of the Christian Mind' (op. cit., p. 257, quoting George Vass, *Understanding Karl Rahner* 2.48).

A dualist is someone who maintains that there are two distinct substances. As we will see in Chapter 18 of this book, dualists maintain that human beings are made up of a soul and a body and neither of these can be reduced to the other. To say that Christians are dualists is to maintain that God and the world are distinct: God created the world and that world and God are not the same. This is, of course, a traditional Christian position.

Lash refers to God as holy mystery (p. 243ff.) in place of Rahner's Holy Mystery (the absence of the capital letters are significant as for Lash God is not an 'other', rather God is *only* to be found in relations in the world, p. 252). I believe that Lash's position can be interpreted as being effectively anti-realist although not many others agree with me!

Lash claims that

> in action and discourse patterned by the frame of reference provided by the creed, we learn to find God in all life, all freedom, all creativity and vitality, and in each particular beauty, each unexpected attainment of relationship and community ... To speak of 'spirit' as 'God' is to ascribe all creativity and conversion, all fresh life and freedom, to divinity. (p. 257)

It is my claim that we have here an apparently clear alignment of Lash with others who effectively see 'religious experience' as having to do with the way in which we learn to look at the world. The words 'patterned by the frame of reference provided by the creed' shows the language game within which one 'learns to find God', in other words in adopting a framework which includes God, we learn within that framework to ascribe relationships and community to God. I do not claim that Lash is or is not an anti-realist, only that his account of religious experience is compatible with an anti-realist account.

There is a modern movement in theology and spirituality which has become so fashionable that it excludes almost all alternatives and that is to see God in all things. Now it is one thing to say that God is the cause of all things, or to say that God can be found through all things (including suffering) but another to say that God is *in* all things. This latter claim makes me want to ask, 'What, including child abuse or rape?' And if God is, indeed, in all things the answer to these questions must be 'yes'. Whilst I would accept that God can be found through suffering, this is not the same as saying that God is *in* suffering. The claim that God is to be found in the everyday world is not a new one – St Francis of Assisi and many others have pointed this out, but this is not Lash's claim.

If Lash's claim were that William James had unduly restricted the possibility of human knowledge of God to direct, personal encounter and that, as well as this, God can be experienced in and through creation, then the point would be well taken. After all St Francis of Assisi, St Ignatius of Loyola and many others have endorsed the view that God can be experienced in creation as well as directly through mystical experiences. However, this is not Lash's claim. By restricting the possibility of 'god' being experienced to mediated experience, he effectively degrades God to the level of an aspect of the world, one which may be affirmed within the frame of reference of belief but has no reference outside this. This may be valid, but James' case, as well as that of Francis of Assisi and other great mystics, is that it is not.

Summary

The Argument from Religious Experience is, I suggest, going to depend to a very large extent on one's presuppositions. If one's presuppositions favour particular types of experiences, one is likely to be convinced by reports of them. If one is a sceptic one will need a great deal of convincing.

If St Paul's experience on the Damascus road (surely the best-known of all religious experiences) is taken as the paradigm example it can be noted that the three accounts of the experience given in the Acts of the Apostles differ quite markedly (Acts chapters 9, 22 and 26). Millions have found Paul's accounts persuasive, millions more have not. There are, of course, some tests that can be applied to any claim to a religious experience. For instance, we can ask whether the experience has had a major influence on the life of the person claiming it. Or we can ask whether it fits in with other thinkers we claim to know from within our tradition. But by referring to 'our tradition' we are already bringing our own preconceptions to bear on the matter.

Religious experiences normally occur within faith rather than act as a foundation for faith. For the individual a particularly vivid experience may constitute a turning point in his or her life. This certainly happened to St Paul. Many others, however, saw Jesus and chose to ignore his message. Someone's claim to have had a religious experience should properly be met by a great deal more scepticism than Swinburne or Davis allow for. The creator God may well exist and some people may indeed experience God's loving presence, but there seems no convincing reason why others should accept their reports unless they are convinced on other grounds that it is reasonably likely that this God exists.

Of course, if there is a God who does appear directly or indirectly to individuals, then this is going to be either the wholly simple, timeless or the everlasting, suffering God. Interestingly, Nicholas Lash in his book *Easter in Ordinary*, although affirming a creator God, rejects the possibility of this God appearing in any extraordinary way to human beings. Lash says that God is instead to be found only in the ordinary things in life. If Lash is right, and I am not at all sure that he is, this places even greater weight on the individual's interpretation of his or her experience and hence, again, on his or her existing presuppositions.

Questions for consideration

a) How would you define a religious experience?

b) If someone claims to have had a religious experience, is this any more or less likely to be true than someone who claims to have seen a flying saucer? Why?

c) If someone claims to have been told by God in a graveyard to murder young women, might this claim be true? Why?

d) Why is Swinburne's argument from religious experience seen as a cumulative argument?

e) Do you consider that religious experience points to the existence of God? Why?

f) What is the difference between William James' and Nicholas Lash's understanding of religious experience?

ELEVEN
Reformed Epistemology

In the second section the difference between realism and anti-realism was explained. Crucial to this distinction was that realists maintain that claims about God are true because they correspond or refer to the reality of God which is independent of the universe God created and sustained. Anti-realists reject correspondence and instead maintain that religious statements are true within the 'story' that religious believers have created. People do not discover religious truths, Gareth Moore says, they make them. In other words, people create religious stories and claims within these stories are true dependent on the grammar of the form of life and language game they inhabit. Don Cupitt says that he is a Christian priest because he lives by the fiction of the Christian story, his point being that Christianity is a made-up story that gives life meaning in a universe that would otherwise be meaningless. There is no reference to a God who creates and sustains the universe, rather, 'God exists' is true within the stories that Christian, Jewish and Islamic believers live by.

If anti-realism is to be rejected, then the realist has to argue on what basis claims about God can be said to refer.

In previous chapters in this section we have looked at the Cosmological, the Ontological, and the Design and Religious Experience arguments for the existence of God. If any of these succeeds in establishing reference to the God who creates and sustains the universe, then the realist case has been established. However, most philosophers do not think the arguments succeed – if by 'succeed' is meant that they establish the existence of God to someone who does not already believe. If this is accepted and the arguments for God's existence cannot establish reference, then what other means does the realist have available to show that his or her truth claims *do* refer? One way of doing this is to appeal to revelation rather than rational argument, and it is this position for which Reformed Epistemologists argue.

Reformed Epistemology gets its name because it comes from within the Reformed Christian tradition. Advocates of this approach mainly come from the United States and include Alvin Plantinga, Cornelius Van Til and Nicholas Wolterstorff. This approach rejects the use of reason advocated by Natural Theology to attempt to prove that language about God successfully refers, as it claims that no justification for belief in God is required. The aim of Reformed Epistemology is to show that it is *rational* not to seek justification for belief in God.

Reformed Epistemology holds that the truth of 'God exists' is not arrived at by a process of argument. Instead, the believer is directly aware of God's presence or of God speaking to him or her through the Bible. Just as I do not need to prove that I am in the presence of my closest friends so the religious believer needs no proof that she is in the presence of God. Belief in God is, thus, a 'properly basic' belief which does not stand in need of justification or proof.

Alvin Plantinga writes:

the mature believer ... does not typically accept belief in God tentatively, or hypothetically, or until something better comes along. Nor, I think, does he accept it as a conclusion from other things he believes; he accepts it as basic, as part of the foundations of his noetic structure. The mature theist commits himself to belief in God, this means that he accepts belief in God as basic ... there is nothing contrary to reason or irrational in so doing ('Is Belief in God Rational?' in C. F. Delaney, ed., *Rationality and Religious Belief*, University of Notre Dame Press, 1979, p. 27).

Nicholas Wolterstorff makes a similar point when he says that 'The Christian scholar ought to allow the belief content of his authentic

Christian commitment to function as his control within his devising and weighing of theories.' (*Faith and Rationality: Reason and Belief in God*, University of Notre Dame Press, 1983.) In other words, belief in God is not subject to rational evaluation; rather it is the individual's believe in God which should be the yardstick by which other beliefs are judged.

Reformed Epistemologists maintain that *it is rational to believe without any rational justification*. To put it another (and more complicated!) way, religious believers are justified in holding that belief in God is 'properly basic' within their noetic structure as their noetic structure is properly ordered. 'Noetic structure' here means the whole structure of a person's knowledge and beliefs. To hold that these beliefs are 'properly basic' means to maintain that they do not require any rational justification. Reformed Epistemologists would claim that proving the existence of anything in any field depends on some presuppositions, for instance the reliability of perception or our other senses. They, it is claimed, can properly rely on the existence of God as one of their bedrock presuppositions.

The obvious charge against this is that some people do not accept the truth of 'God exists', whereas most people (although, it must be accepted, not all philosophers) accept the reliability of our senses. The reply to this by the Reformed Epistemologist will be that believers have a 'properly ordered noetic structure'. In other words, *they* see the world correctly whereas non-believers do not. Reformed Epistemologists do not seek to justify this claim, if they did they would be embarking on another form of Natural Theology which they have already rejected. Instead, they explain why they see the world correctly and others do not. They may, for instance, say that non-believers are prevented from seeing the world as it really is due to pride or the 'noetic effects of sin'. Sin has adversely affected their ability to see the reality of God. Non-believers, therefore, cannot be convinced by rational argument since this is to appeal to human reason and human reason is precisely unable to arrive at the existence of God. Instead, God's grace must be prayed for so that individuals may come to 'see the world rightly'.

Nicholas Wolterstorff seeks to shift the balance from scepticism towards claims about God to holding that these claims should be accepted unless there is evidence against them. He says:

> A person is rationally justified in believing a certain proposition which he does believe unless he has adequate reason to cease from believing it. Our beliefs are rational unless we have reason from refraining (from belief) ... They are innocent until proved guilty, not guilty until proved innocent ('Can Belief in God be Rational if it has no Foundations?', ibid., p. 163).

Reformed Epistemology shares with Natural Theology a realist conviction, namely that 'God exists' is true if and only if this correctly refers to the God on which the universe depends. However, unlike Natural Theology it does *not* use arguments to establish that religious language successfully refers to God. Faith alone is all that is required and those with faith should not feel discomforted because they cannot provide rational grounds for their faith. Plantinga accepts that religious beliefs can be defeated if there are arguments which show that any set of beliefs is not rationally tenable. However, these 'defeaters' (such as the challenge posed by the problem of evil) can themselves be defeated if reasons can be given which would undermine the challenge they pose.

Unfortunately, the counter-argument is self-evident, namely that *any* group can claim that they are rationally justified in believing *anything*, simply on the ground that they are right and others are wrong. They could admit the possibility of error but could explain away anything that looked, to non-believers, like a convincing challenge. The following example may illustrate the point. My family and friends may believe that the donkey in the field we once owned where we lived in Devon was the daughter of the Great-Donkey-in-the-Sky who created the universe. They may feel convinced that they are called to erect a Donkey temple to Her honour. They may say those who reject this belief have sinned against animals and cannot see the truth of the Great-Donkey revelation, and that this is due to the effects of sin on their ability to see the truth (perhaps they have eaten meat or been cruel to animals). They may say that they do not need to justify their belief and that they are justified in believing it to be true without any form of rational argument at all. They may claim that, as realists, what makes their belief true is that there is, indeed, a Great-Donkey-in-the-Sky who is the mother of the donkey in the field and if there is no such Great-Donkey then they would be mistaken, but they may nevertheless be firmly convinced that they are right and that they alone have the truth. They may even say that they are aware of the presence of the Great-Donkey on moonlit nights when she gallops with her daughter.

The point of the Great-Donkey example is that unless the Reformed Epistemologists can provide rational grounds which would be acceptable both to Great-Donkey worshippers and to others for choosing one revelation rather than another, there seems to be no basis to their claim. Reformed Epistemology comes from the United States where Protestant Christianity is particularly strong, but the Reformed Epistemologist provides no grounds as to why the Christian revelation should be accepted rather than, say, that of Islam. Islam is, after all, the fastest growing religion in the world and it recognises Jesus as a prophet sent by God. Islam recognises Mary as a virgin mother. It recognises the great prophets of the Hebrew Scriptures through whom God is claimed to work; however, it maintains that the final revelation by Allah was given to Mohammed through the dictation of the Holy Koran. Unless Reformed Epistemologists can provide adequate criteria for accepting Christian claims to revelation rather than the Islamic (or any other) claims then its argument is circular as it is effectively arguing to legitimise an existing conviction.

The anti-realist approach is *similar* to the Reformed Epistemologist's in that it rejects all attempts at justifying or proving the existence of God. It also holds that it is rational to believe without justification – indeed, it maintains that it is a mistake to look for justification. There comes a point when talk of justification comes to an end and we just accept a practice within a given form of life. However, the anti-realist differs from the Reformed Epistemologist on the issue of truth:

- The Reformed Epistemologist is a realist – he or she maintains that statements are true because they successfully refer to God.
- Anti-realists maintain that statements are true because they cohere or fit in with other true statements within a particular form of life. Theology is only 'grammar', the grammar of a particular language game.

This is a vital distinction and the consequences are considerable. As we shall see later, the understanding of central religious ideas such as miracles, petitionary prayer and eternal life will be very different for the realist and the anti-realist (see Chapters 15, 17 and 18).

The problem for the realist is that establishing reference seems impossible and a faith claim to reference, in a world where there are many religious faiths, seems inadequate.

Questions for consideration

a) What is a 'noetic structure'?
b) Why do Reformed Epistemologists consider that they do not need to justify their beliefs?
c) What is the difference between a Reformed Epistemologist and an anti-realist?
d) What are the chief problems the Reformed Epistemologist faces in claiming reference? Can these be overcome?

TWELVE

Answering the Anti-Realist Challenge

In this section of the book we have reviewed some of the arguments for the existence of God and seen that they all depend on presuppositions believers are likely to accept and about which non-believers are likely to be dubious. In the last chapter, the alternative approach of Reformed Epistemology was examined and it, also, seems to rest on flimsy grounds. However, this confronts those who want to maintain a realist claim to the truth of religious beliefs with a very real problem: how can they maintain that their beliefs refer when there seems to be no adequate basis to justify the claim to reference?

Where does the realist go? Natural Theology, which attempts to argue for the existence of God using the arguments we have considered, seems to rest on assumptions that can be challenged by the non-believer and that will only commend themselves to those who already believe. The Reformed Epistemologist's position amounts to little more than saying that the believer is rationally justified in accepting her own presuppositions in spite of her inability to demonstrate this. The anti-realist seems to hold most of the philosophic cards and reason might seem to propel the believer towards the anti-realist camp as no justification is required and truth is internal to the different forms of life. The Christian, Muslim, Jew, Hindu, Sikh or Buddhist verifies belief by reference to their own framework and there is no independent standard of truth.

This, in my view, is the major challenge facing theology in the next century. Many theologians do not wish to accept the consequences of the anti-realist position but they have few arguments to demonstrate that this position is mistaken. There are no easy or convincing answers.

However, whilst the anti-realist approach appears to have great strengths it also suffers from significant weaknesses. It maintains that within a particular religious form of life there is no doubt about the central claims of faith and it leaves little room for an agonising search for God or for the real experience of the 'absence of God' felt by many religious believers at key times in their lives. It rejects God's activity in the world in terms of answered prayer or miracles (see pp. 174ff. and 205) or the claim that mystics and saints claim to live in an 'I/Thou' relationship with God. Anti-realists will also reject the idea of the individual surviving death (p. 221). This position may, therefore, be accused of distorting the nature of the claims being made by religious believers.

Wittgenstein said that philosophy should 'leave everything as it is' – it was, he maintained, the task of philosophy to understand and to clarify, not to lay down what could and could not be said or believed. Many anti-realists claim to be supporters of Wittengestein but in this key respect they depart from his views: they are prescriptive.

More significantly, there seems to be a verificationist/positivist assumption lurking under the anti-realist position. This means that they seem to assume that unless a statement is verifiable or provable it is meaningless. Anti-realists draw an implicit distinction between two types of statement:

1 *Empirical statements* that must be verifiable and that are about states of affairs that are independent of language such as tables, chairs and bookcases; and

2 *Grammatical statements* that are true within a particular form of life but find their meaning and their truth only within the form of life (prime numbers would be a good example; see. p. 61)

Anti-realists often claim that statements about God are not 'empirical statements' because they cannot be verified. They must, therefore, be 'only grammatical statements'.

This is not a position that Wittgenstein took, yet some of his disciples seem to accept it without question. Wittgenstein left open the possibility that empirical statement may not be verifiable but still be true in a realist sense. Wittgenstein did not concern himself with the realist/anti-realist distinction. Instead, he aimed to leave people's beliefs largely untouched and attempted to understand them. He left open the possibility that religious statements may refer to God or a transcendent order even though this cannot be verified. Wittgenstein tried to clarify what religious believers said and warned of the danger of interpreting religious language in terms of some other language (such as chemistry). He was trying to draw attention to the complexities and sophistication of religious language and that is all. Wittgenstein, unlike the anti-realist, was very modest in his aims and in what he thought that philosophy could achieve. He certainly did *not* claim that religious statements were 'only' grammatical.

The initial plausibility of the anti-realist position may, therefore, be challenged once it is recognised that it is based on a verificationist assumption which can be rejected. However, the realist's problem remains: how to establish reference or how to justify the claim that language about God refers in a world where there are many competing religious claims.

In praise of modesty

Religious believers are frequently absolutely convinced that they are right. Whether it be militant Hindus in India; fundamentalist Muslims in Iran, the Sudan, Egypt, Palestine or Saudi Arabia; Orthodox Jews in Israel; Protestants in Northern Ireland; Southern Baptists in the USA or Roman Catholic bodies such as Opus Dei or branches of the Catholic Magisterium in Rome, each has a conviction that *it* has the truth, it alone is right and others are either wrong or, at least, see less of the truth.

It is not just religious organisations that are convinced of the rightness of their views. Individual theologians or religious leaders are just as convinced. The passion and conviction of Karl Barth, Don

Cupitt, Thomas Aquinas, Martin Luther, Ian Paisley, Pope John Paul II and many others is self-evident, and humility about the truth is not a hallmark of any of their dogmatic views.

Some theologians today have little comprehension of the philosophic problems they need to face and the consequences of the positions they would wish to adopt. Most of them would claim to be realists. They are each convinced that they have the truth and it therefore follows that others who disagree with them will either be mistaken or, at least, will have less of the truth than they do. However, they do not appreciate a crucial philosophic insight: If one is a realist about the truth, it should necessarily follow that one should be humble about one's claim to truth, as any philosophic realist *must* be prepared to admit that he or she may be wrong.

Anti-realists may, legitimately, be totally sure *they* have the truth as on their definition truth simply *is* the truth held within a certain form of life. Within their form of life what they hold as true *is* true. The anti-realist Catholic will be entirely justified in being 100 per cent sure he is right provided he adheres to the dictates of the Magisterium as, by definition, what the Magisterium says *is* the truth, for the Magisterium determines the rules of the language game. Anti-realism offers a security and certainty that is not available to the realist. The realist Catholic, by contrast, may *believe* that her Church has the truth, but she will know that she and the Church could be wrong and that those statements she holds to be true may fail to correspond to the ultimate state of the universe. She must, therefore, be modest.

It is one thing to believe that your group has the ultimate religious truth and to stake your life on this belief. This may involve passion and self-sacrifice, it may well be costly and may bring you suffering and opposition from others, but this is your choice, freely made and freely adhered to. From a religious point of view, it is the freedom of this assent and the actions this choice leads to that are often held to be meritorious. *However*, it is one thing to take such truths on yourself – it is quite another to impose them on others.

A Southern Baptist in the USA may be convinced that his faith is true and his understanding of Christianity is correct. A Catholic may be convinced that the Magisterium in Rome has access to the truth and that documents like *Veritatis Splendor* (1993) set out certain actions which are 'intrinsically evil'. The Muslim may be convinced that to die in a holy war is a guarantee of entry to paradise. They may each base their lives on their understanding and risk ridicule and opposition from others who do not share this belief. However, once a person turns from a passionate concern with his personal commitment to what he regards as ultimate truth, then he transgresses an important boundary line. Once, for instance, he rejects homosexuals as 'sinners', or those who have an abortion after rape as 'wicked and debased', or those who do not accept his morality as 'evil', then he is imposing his convictions on other people. If he is a realist, he must admit that he could be wrong and to impose his own certainties with the knowledge that his certainties may be mistaken is morally unacceptable. Gentle persuasion and argument may be the most that is morally permissible.

The pursuit of truth matters tremendously. But humility, gentleness, compassion, love, forgiveness and concern for others may be even more important. Religious belief should call individuals to take these values on board and to live them out in service to and love for others, even at great personal cost. When we lose sight of this in our rush to judge others on the basis of certainty about objective truth, we may lose sight of the most important thing of all.

In the next section we turn from consideration of whether God exists, and what this means, to look at some of the attributes claimed for God. These will be seen to give rise to their own problems.

Questions for consideration

a) What might it mean to say that anti-realism is based on an implicit verificationist assumption?

b) What might a believer who is a realist claim is lost, if one holds to an anti-realist position?

c) What is the chief problem the realist faces when faced with the anti-realist challenge?

GOD'S POWER
AND KNOWLEDGE

THIRTEEN

Omnipotence

Religious believers claim that God is almighty. Emphasis on God's power is important so that God's providential care should not be in any way limited by lack of power. Certain of Jesus' miracles were specifically intended to show that, like God, he too had power over the physical universe: he changed water into wine and 'even the winds and the waves obeyed him'.

However, once we start to examine the claim that God can do anything, we encounter some complications. These complications are not just the province of philosophers interested in picking holes in religious belief – almost all teenagers who have any interest in religion will be aware of them. Some examples will show the problems that are involved. They are examples which most readers will find familiar, as they probably heard them during their schooldays:

1 If God can do anything, can he commit suicide?

2 Can God swim? A six-year-old can swim, so if God cannot do so, this seems a clear limitation to his power.

3 Can God sin? Many of us do this all the time, so if God can do everything, He should be able to do this as well.

4 Can God make an object which is too heavy for God to lift? I can do this with the aid of a concrete mixer, some sand and cement, but it would seem that whatever answer we give in the case of God necessarily limits God's power. If God cannot create such an object, then God cannot do something that a human being can do. But if

God can create such a thing, then there is something that God cannot do, namely lift the object.

5 Can God make an object so that it is completely black all over and at the same time white all over? Alternatively, can God make a square circle?

6 Can God swear by a being greater than God? If God cannot do this, then there is something God cannot do. If God can do this, then there must be a being greater than God.

A definition is needed which enables these problems to be resolved. There are various possibilities and they will be dealt with in turn:

Definition One: God can do absolutely anything, including the logically impossible.

On this view, God can do all of the above. God can do things that are contradictory; God can do the nonsensical; God can create square circles, commit suicide and swim. God can even make a stone that is too heavy for God to lift – *and then go on to lift it!* God is not limited by the laws of logic, since God created these laws and could abolish them if he wished to do so.

The French philosopher René Descartes maintained something close to this position, and it is the strongest affirmation of God's power. Descartes considered that if God had to conform to the laws of logic and non-contradiction, this would be a limit on God's absolute power. He held that God created this world with its laws of logic but God would have been capable of creating different universes within different laws of logic. We simply have no idea, according to Descartes, of what is and what is not possible for God, so we cannot lay down any limitations on God's absolute omnipotence.

To say God can do absolutely anything is an approach that is sometimes taken by believers who have never really thought through the problems that arise. Such individuals need to take seriously the fact that even the Bible accepts that there are things God cannot do. It says, for example, that God is not able to lie or swear by a being greater than God (Hebrews 6:13,18).

The view that God can do the logically impossible is incoherent and, if it were true, would show that God would not be worth worshipping. Such a God could lie and deceive, God could swear to reward the virtuous and then condemn them to everlasting torment. Even if such a view were possible, this could not be a God worth worshipping.

Logic and the laws of contradiction mark the limits to what it makes sense to say. It is meaningless to talk of square circles. Nothing could be a square circle. If it were a square it would not be a circle and if it were a circle it would not be a square. It is true, of course, that God could arrange some strange geometric figure and call this a square circle, but God would then be making up a private language of God's own – certainly God would not have created what we mean by a square circle. This, however, is no limitation on God's power since instead of 'square circle' being a task God cannot do, it is a meaningless utterance, as it has no content.

Even more telling than this, however, is the fact that a God who could do the logically impossible would be fundamentally evil. This can be shown by the following argument.

One of the most effective arguments to justify belief in an all-good and all-powerful God in the face of much evil and suffering in the world is the *free will defence* (see my *The Puzzle of Evil*). This argument claims that God allows human beings free will in order that they may be free to love God and to show love to their neighbours. Love requires freedom; love is only possible if freedom exists. A person who is not free is unable to love. A robot could mimic the actions of love, but this would not be the same as genuine love.

If, therefore, human beings are to love they must be free, and if they are free they have to have the power to be free to choose to do dreadful things on some occasions. Events such as the slaughter of the Poles, homosexuals, Gipsies and Jews in the Nazi concentration camps, the killings in Stalin's death camps and the massacres carried out by the Pol Pot regime in Cambodia, by the Hutus in Rwanda or by the Serbs in Kosovo are all examples of human free will being used to inflict massive suffering. The free will defence maintains that God would not interfere to stop these tragedies without taking away human freedom. Human freedom is such an important gift from God that the price of suffering is held to be worth it. Only if we are free can we enter into love-relationships with each other and with God.

However, if God could do the logically impossible, then God could bring about two mutually contradictory states of affairs. God could have created a world such that

1 Human beings would have the genuine free will that they now possess, and
2 These free beings could be controlled in such a way that they would only act justly, kindly and rightly.

Now these two positions are contradicions. A person cannot *both* be completely free to choose how he or she will act *and at the same time* be controlled so that he or she always acts rightly. The two cannot go together; that would amount to logical nonsense. However, if God can do the logically impossible, then there would be no problem in God doing the logically nonsensical. According to this view of omnipotence, God *could* have created this ideal state of affairs (Ninian Smart refers to it as 'the Utopian thesis') whereby complete freedom and goodness would be combined. God's failure to bring about this state of affairs shows that he must be malevolent and, effectively, be playing with human beings. All the evils that men have inflicted on other men and women could have been avoided, and at no cost.

However, because God cannot do the logically impossible this is an impossible state of affairs. God could

1 *Either* control us so that we would always act rightly, in which case we would not be free, or
2 God could give us freedom, in which case humans must be able to do evil.

Another definition of omnipotence is therefore needed.

Definition Two: God can do everything that is logically possible.

This seems attractive, but this definition of omnipotence is not adequate either. The examples given at the beginning of the chapter illustrate the problems. It is certainly logically possible for a six-year-old to swim, but if God is wholly simple and timeless and does not have a body this is likely to be impossible for God – although, of course, Jesus may well have swum in the lake when he was a child. (This raises questions as to whether it is logically possible for a literally timeless God to become a human being. However, such questions would involve us discussing Christology, and we do not have space for that here.) It is certainly logically possible for a human person to commit suicide or to sin, just as it is logically possible to make an object that is too heavy to lift.

If, therefore, omnipotence is defined as 'the power to do everything that is logically possible', then God will have to be able to do things which the believer often wants to say God cannot do (like evil, lying, committing suicide or even committing adultery). A further modification of the definition is, therefore, required.

Definition Three: God can do everything that is absolutely possible

This was the definition given by St Thomas Aquinas (*Summa Theologiae* 1.25.4) and it is probably the most satisfactory one. Aquinas defined what is 'absolutely possible' in terms of anything that does not involve a contradiction. So if we said 'God can X', then for Aquinas this would be true provided that whatever is substituted as 'X' does not involve a contradiction. Two types of contradiction are possible:

1 A contradiction within the task ('X'). Thus if 'X' was 'create a square circle' this would be held to be impossible as a square circle is a contradiction. God cannot, therefore, do a contradictory task.

This would rule out 'X' being 'create free human beings who are also determined' as this would also be a contradiction.

2 A contradiction between the task ('X') and God. Thus if 'X' was 'die' then this would be a contradiction since if God is wholly simple, timeless and spaceless, then God could not change in order to go out of existence. God could not swim nor could God swear by a being greater than God since both these would contradict the nature of God.

This is highly satisfactory as a definition as it maintains God's absolute power and only rules out God being able to do something which is not even a task at all since it is just words which look as though they are describing a task, but in fact are not (e.g. square circle). The only restriction on God's power is God's own nature which prevents God doing evil, dying, etc.

However, there is a problem that goes to the very heart of the idea of God as wholly simple. *If* this model of God is adopted and *if* Aquinas' definition is used, then the question arises 'Can God choose?' At first sight, of course, the answer would appear to be 'of course', but it is not as easy as that. Aquinas' definition rules out any task that contradicts God's nature. To choose involves change and, therefore, if God is utterly unchangeable (as God must be if God is timeless) this would seem to rule out choice as choice involves change and potential. We have already seen (p. 33) that the wholly simple and timeless God is held to have no potential.

The only way round this problem would be to say that God can timelessly choose. But does this make sense? Does it not belong to the very nature of choice that there must be a time before and after the choice? If this is so, then 'timeless choice' would be a logical contradiction and would have to be ruled out. Of course one could retreat behind mystery, but to plead 'mystery' just at the point when philosophic argument gets difficult is certainly not philosophically acceptable. This issue appears inconsequential but in fact is crucially important as *if* the wholly simple and timeless God cannot choose, then God could not act other than as God does act. God has no freedom. This would have grave consequences.

There is one particular act which God is held to perform which could be rendered impossible if God cannot choose; this is creation. God is held to have created the universe from nothing. Aquinas, interestingly, did not think that this could be proved philosophically and considered that creation was a revealed truth and it could be that he appeals to revelation because the philosophic problems seem insurmountable.

Augustine considered the question 'What did God do before the creation of the universe?' and came to the conclusion that the question was absurd. Time came into existence with the creation of the universe and before creation there was no time. God existed timelessly, and for timeless God time does not pass. To ask about events before time came into existence is, therefore, nonsensical. On the surface, this seems reasonable.

Let us, however, try an exercise in imagination, albeit a very difficult one, as it is an attempt to imagine the unimaginable. Imagine that the creation has not yet taken place. God timelessly exists. There is no matter, no celestial beings, no time – nothing other than timeless God, for whom time does not pass. So we have timeless God, existing without any time frame at all, and nothing beyond God.

The problem is that if there is no time frame at all, how can the universe come into existence? If the creation is to take place, the universe must begin to exist. God must, timelessly, do the equivalent of saying, 'Let there be light' (Genesis 1:3). There is, however, no moment at which this can be said, even timelessly, because there is no time for God. *There seem to be two alternatives:*

1 *Either* the universe must be necessary and must always have existed because the wholly simple and timeless God could not bring it into existence (in which case, although God may sustain it and keep it in existence, God cannot have created it – a position taken by Schleiermacher), or
2 If God did create the universe, then God must be in time in order

to do so and, therefore, the claim that God is timeless has to be rejected. Unless there is some time frame in God himself, unless God is essentially temporal, there can be no time at which the decision is made that the universe must come into existence.

It will not do, on this point, to claim that the creation is a doctrine revealed by God as Aquinas does. If God is literally timeless, then it would seem that God *cannot*, logically, have created the universe from nothing. God could, certainly, have sustained a universe which had always existed. However, God could not have created this universe in the absence of a time frame.

If timeless choice is possible, then God could choose to create. God could move from non-creation to creation without a time frame, without changing and without actualising any potential. It is far from clear whether this is possible.

There is not space to pursue this argument in detail here, but the alternatives lie between saying:

1. It is a contradiction in God's nature to say that a wholly simple, timeless God can choose, so choice is not possible for this model of God. This would then force us *either* to hold that God has to act whenever God acts and God is wholly determined by God's nature and therefore is not free *or* to abandon entirely the idea of a wholly simple, timeless God and switch to an everlasting, suffering God for whom choice is not a problem as God is in time.

2. To be able to show that 'timeless choice' does not involve a contradiction. This would mean arguing that timeless God has 'timeless potential' perhaps by saying that, although God cannot be changed by being acted upon, God can change within God's self. If this option is to be followed then sense has to be made of timeless change, and this is not easy.

Both alternatives are problematic!

Before leaving the issue of the omnipotence of a creator God, one final definition needs consideration:

Definition Four: God has all the logically possible powers that are possible for God to have

Anthony Kenny, in *The God of the Philosophers* (Penguin, 1979, p. 98) expresses this definition of omnipotence with greater precision:

> Divine omnipotence, therefore, if it is to be a coherent notion, must be something less than the complete omnipotence which is the possession of all logically possible powers. It must be a narrower omnipotence, consisting in the possession of all logically possible powers which it is logically possible for a being with the attributes of God to possess.

The first point to note is that this is very different from Aquinas' definition as it defines omnipotence in terms of God's *powers*. Aquinas always resists this, preferring to define omnipotence in terms of God's actions. The distinction is important as Aquinas does not consider that God has potential, God has no unactualised powers. However, if God is in time (a position Aquinas rejects) then Kenny's definition becomes persuasive. An everlasting, suffering God can, indeed, have powers which God does not use and God can have powers which are used on some occasions and not on others. For instance, God could both have the power to make an irresistible wind and an unmoveable tree. What God could not do would be to actualise both at the same time as then there would be a contradiction!

Definition Five: To talk of God's omniscience is to talk of the irresistible power of love.

We have looked at four definitions of God's omniscience, all of which rest on a realist understanding about claims that God exists. In other words, they depend on there existing a Being or Substance called 'God' who acts in the universe. God may be either wholly simple and timeless or the everlasting, suffering God and different definitions may be appropriate for each model. There remains the problem of how omniscience would be defined if God exists as a reality within the form of life of the believing community. Because God is not a being or spirit who can act in the universe, it would seem at first sight that any talk of God acting would be meaningless, but this is too simplistic. St Teresa of Avila (1512–82) is said to have written the following lines:

> *Christ has no body now on earth but yours,*
> *No hands but yours, no feet but yours,*
> *Yours are the only eyes through which He is to look*
> *with compassion on the world,*
> *Yours are the feet with which He is to go about doing good,*
> *And yours the hands with which He is to bless us now.*

The picture St Teresa presents here (different pictures are presented elsewhere in her writings) is not of a creator God who is continuously active in the world: She says God has no other hands but ours, no other feet but ours. It is we, therefore, who must do the acting on behalf of God. It is we who must act for God and show compassion to the world. It is we who must go out among the poor and the weak to show them God's compassion, and the blessing with which we bless others must be the blessing of our love and care.

To talk of God's action, therefore, is to talk of our action. God's action is found wherever in the world we find compassion, wherever we find love, wherever the poor are provided for, wherever those in prison are visited, wherever the sick are cared for and the weak are supported and helped.

We do not need, however, to think in terms of a wholly simple and timeless God or an everlasting God who in some unknowable way acts through people. Rather, acts of compassion and love *are*

God's actions, that is what we call acts of compassion and love. This is a powerful and attractive picture. God's actions are seen wherever the power of love is at work.

However, this is a revisionary view. St Teresa does not actually want to go as far as the revisionists want to go. She wants to show that human beings cannot rely on God to act, and that we must act on behalf of God. She is not suggesting that God *cannot* or *does not* act. For Teresa, as for mainstream Christianity, God certainly can act directly in the world without human agency – it is just that believers must not rely on this intervention. She would also want to say that God does truly act through people; she would not want to imply that what we call God's actions are really just the acts of individuals behaving in a certain way.

To talk of God's omnipotence, in this view, is to argue that a different way of living life is possible which can triumph over adversity. It is possible for human beings to live life so that any individual can overcome the trivialization of his or her life. Socrates said the lover of the good cannot be harmed. This means nothing can take away from him or her the inner orientation towards kindness, love and virtue which is the most important part of his or her life. To be sure, such individuals can lose possessions and suffer pain and even death, but since the most important thing in their lives is the way they live and the path of holiness that they follow, they cannot really be hurt in any important sense.

Gandhi might be a good example here. He showed that the path of peace, of non-violence, can overcome all opposition. Gandhi was killed, but his killer could not overcome the life and example Gandhi showed. The Anglican Archbishop of Uganda, killed by Idi Amin, in the end helped to defeat the general by his example and the inspiration he gave Christians in the country. Nelson Mandela, locked up for over 25 years by the South African government on Robbin Island, and released in 1990 became a recognised international figure and a key element in the future of his country in spite of having no power and being completely subject to the South African authorities. Similarly, the might and power of the Warsaw Pact and the control exercised by Stalinist Communism over so many millions in Eastern Europe was overcome not by force of arms, but by largely peaceful and popular movements.

Kruschev, the former President of the USSR, apparently asked, 'How many divisions has the Pope?' as a way of mocking the powerlessness of the Church. And yet it is the Church that in country after country around the world provides the inspiration for the poor and the weak and helps to bring about a more equal and fair society. To talk of omnipotence can be to talk of the power to overcome even death because, if we will only follow the path of holiness, death cannot trivialise our lives.

It is in these senses that the path of sanctity can be one of omnipotence. Even if people die in a just cause, they have overcome death, as their lives have not been rendered meaningless by their passing away. The phrase *Amor vincit omnia* (Love conquers all) claims love is omnipotent since love can overcome even the strongest foe.

Omnipotence, therefore, does not need to be the power exercised by a God who created the world and still controls it. Rather, talk of omnipotence seeks to draw people to the invincible power of love found in weakness, humility and selflessness. Such omnipotence can be enjoyed by the poorest of the poor, but generally not by the rich – they have too much to lose. Their possessions can get in between them and the Kingdom of God, as the possessions of the rich young man in the Christian Gospels prevented him from following Jesus. The Kingdom of God is to be built on earth, and the builders are those who seek to live out lives of love in the midst of a world dedicated largely to materialism and self-interest.

To be sure, this is a revisionary understanding of omnipotence, but it is nevertheless a plausible one. The insight into the power of holiness, peace and self-giving love that it shows is valid. Those who maintain talk of omnipotence is about an all-powerful, timeless and everlasting God need to ask themselves, anti-realists would claim, what is gained by such talk.

Summary

What is meant by talk of God's omnipotence will vary depending on whether the word 'God' refers (1) to a wholly simple, timeless substance, (2) to an everlasting, suffering God or (3) to the God who exists within the form of life of the believing community.

1 If God is wholly simple and timeless the most plausible definition of omnipotence is that God can do anything that is absolutely possible, although the difficulty remains of defining what is absolutely possible. There is also the problem of whether it is possible for this type of God to choose since choice may involve potential.

2 If God is the everlasting, suffering God then God's omnipotence may be best defined in terms of having all logically possible powers.

3 A revisionary understanding of omnipotence is possible whereby omnipotence means the power of love and holiness to overcome in all situations. Omnipotence, on this view, does not refer to the power of a creator God, but to the power inherent in each of us if we would give up living for ourselves and instead devote ourselves to others.

Questions for consideration

a) What is the main problem with the claim that God can do absolutely everything including the logically impossible?
b) Could God commit suicide?
c) Can God choose?
d) Has God got powers that he does not use?
e) What do you consider to be the most satisfactory definition of omnipotence?

FOURTEEN

Omniscience

If omnipotence is one of the most important aspects of the puzzle of God, omniscience is certainly another. God, the believer often maintains, knows everything. God is *omnipresent* (present everywhere throughout God's creation as well as outside of it) and nothing can be hid from God. God has numbered every hair on our heads and knows every sparrow that falls. God's knowledge helps to assure the believer that, as Julian of Norwich put it, 'all shall be well and all manner of things shall be well'. Julian could not see how this was the case, but she trusted in God, and this was at least partly because God's knowledge was not in any way limited.

As always, however, once we start to think seriously about what it means to talk of God knowing everything, complexities and difficulties arise, and much depends on which view of God one adopts. Let us, therefore, look at the possibilities in turn.

a) The wholly simple, timeless omniscient God
The wholly simple, timeless God sees the past, the present and the future simultaneously. This God, we have previously seen, is like an observer on a mountain road looking down on the road and seeing all points on that road at once. Time does not pass for God, since all time is present to God. It follows that every event that has ever happened is simultaneously present to God. The age of the dinosaurs, the empire of Alexander the Great, the Civil War in North America, the arrival of the first settlers in Australia, today and the end of the world are all, alike, present to timeless God.

Supporters of timeless God will, therefore, argue for a very strong version of omniscience. Timeless God knows everything – past, present and future. To God, of course, there is no past, no present and no future, since all temporal events are simultaneously present to God. However, God knows at what point on the road of time our lives lie. Such a God knows our future absolutely, in every detail.

This is an attractive view, but it raises a serious problem. If God knows events that are future to us – even though they are not future to God, because they are timelessly present to God – in what sense can we be free? If God timelessly knows that my 19-year-old son, Luke, will marry a woman called Petunia on her twenty-seventh birthday, has Luke (or Petunia) any choice in the matter?

Put another way, if God knows our future is our future wholly determined, and are we like puppets under the control of a puppet master? Parts of the Christian tradition have implied this. The whole idea of *predestination*, which implies that our lives are determined by God, can be seen as opposed to human freedom. Yet, on the other hand, God is meant to have given us human beings the gift of freedom so that we can choose to turn towards God or away from God. Love requires us to be free, and if our actions are wholly determined and controlled by God, then, apparently, we cannot be free.

There are two alternative ways of presenting God's knowledge:

1 If God knows Y, then necessarily Y will happen (where Y is an event in the world), or
2 If Y happens, then necessarily God knows Y.

These are significantly different. In the first case, it is God's knowledge that causes event Y to happen. In the second case, it is the happening of event Y that causes God to know Y. The first leads to predestination, the second does not. In the first case, what happens in the world happens because God knows it will happen and, therefore, human beings cannot be free in any real sense.

If the wholly simple, timeless God knows our future actions, what sense can be made of the belief that we are free? Boethius (480–524), who was a Consul in ancient Rome, addressed this problem. He was falsely accused and put into gaol, and his sons were similarly treated. His book the *Consolation of Philosophy*, was written in prison as a dialogue between him and his 'kindly nurse, Philosophy', in whose company he had lived since his youth. He complained to 'the Lady Philosophy' that he had been a just and virtuous man, seeking to govern the Roman state fairly. He referred to Plato's injunction (in the *Republic*) that the ideal state should be governed by philosophers who would be wise enough to be genuinely interested in the good of the state. Boethius was a philosopher and had done all he could to govern the state well, and yet his reward was to have his possessions stripped from him and to be thrown into gaol. The book was an attempt to make sense of his plight.

Boethius says to the Lady Philosophy that God knows everything. God therefore knows the future actions of human beings, and this must mean that men and women are not free. However, the Lady Philosophy replies that this is a mistake. God does, indeed, timelessly know what we shall do in the future, but God's knowledge is *not causal*. God timelessly sees our future actions, but what God sees is the result of our freedom, God does not cause us to act in any particular way (this is option 2 above).

On this basis, therefore, God can timelessly know all human actions, past, present and future, without taking away human freedom. Our free actions are what God sees, and God's seeing does not cause us to act in a certain way. God timelessly knows that my son Luke will marry Petunia, but it will be Luke and Petunia who will decide to get married, God will not cause them to do so.

The only problem is that this attractive position is not possible if God is wholly simple and timeless, or at least St Thomas Aquinas maintained it was not possible. For Aquinas, God is not a being with attributes, all God's attributes are identical to each other. God's wisdom, love, justice, knowledge, etc., are all identical in God. God does not depend on the universe for anything. God does not, therefore, know what happens in the universe because these things happen; rather, things happen in the universe because God knows them. God's knowledge, in other words, is causal. Surprising as it may seem, therefore, Aquinas' view of God leads to determinism. Fr. Gerry Hughes SJ makes this clear in his book *The Nature of God* (Routledge, 1995). In the chapter on Divine Omniscience he chronicles the many attempts that have been made to get round the problem. He concludes, rightly in my view, that they all fail. Hughes then puts forward his own view, which is simple but has profound consequences.

Gerry Hughes maintains that since it is absolutely essential to maintain that human beings are genuinely free (defined as 'liberty of indifference', see below), there is no alternative but to say that God's knowledge does not cause events in the universe. God, he maintains, must depend for God's knowledge on what happens in the universe.

The problem with this attractive position is that it means that God's knowledge is no longer identical with God's other attributes and Hughes is therefore forced to modify the idea of divine simplicity. He claims that even if God is dependent on the universe for God's knowledge it is still possible to hold a restricted view of simplicity – but I am not at all sure this is right. Once the simplicity of God is compromised, then God is not simple at all. It is rather like a girl saying, 'I am a little bit pregnant.' Either she is pregnant or she is not; there is no halfway house. Similarly, I suggest, either

1 God is simple in the manner defined by Aquinas and therefore God does not depend for his knowledge on creatures. In this case, God's knowledge causes everything in the universe, *or*

2 The idea of God as wholly simple has to be abandoned and it would be necessary to move to a God who is in time.

Both alternatives suffer from real problems! An example of one of the problems is given on p. 174.

b) The everlasting, suffering, omniscient God

Timeless God knows the past, the present and the future absolutely, as all time is present to God. The position is different, however, with the everlasting God, who is in time. To the everlasting God, the future is future and the past is past. There is no problem with such a God knowing the past and the present completely. The difficulties arise with knowledge of the future.

There is no problem in claiming that the everlasting God can know future events which depend on the present situation in the universe. The everlasting God can know today that the sun will rise tomorrow and the date on which Haley's Comet will return to the Solar System. This information is available to human beings as well, since the celestial events behave according to known laws. Can everlasting God, however, know the future free actions of human beings?

There are two basic possibilities, which depend on the way we define human freedom:

1. *Genuine freedom*: Genuine freedom (termed 'liberty of indifference' by philosophers) is the freedom to act according to our own choices in ways that are not wholly determined by our genetic make-up, upbringing and background. Human beings, on this basis, have a measure of genuine freedom which is not determined by their nature. Obviously, this freedom is restricted – I do not have the freedom to fly out of my window or to make myself invisible and the more we learn about the human genome the more we have to realize that we are heavily influenced by our genetic make-up. Nevertheless, on this view, I do have freedom to make moral choices, and these choices are not entirely determined by my nature.

The everlasting God cannot, if we have genuine freedom, know the future free actions of human beings, as there is no truth there to be known. We are able to choose what to do with our lives, and God cannot *know* what choices will be made. Of course, God may be able to predict the future free choices of human beings with considerable accuracy, but to say that God knows the future necessarily means that God cannot be mistaken. If, therefore, men and women are free (in the way defined here), the everlasting God's omniscience cannot extend to knowledge of the future actions of human beings.

On this basis, the everlasting God can still be held to be omniscient. Such a God knows everything that it is logically possible to know. God thus knows all true propositions about the past and the present, but the future is simply not there to be known. It is, therefore, no limitation on God's omniscience to deny God knowledge of the future actions of human beings, since the future is open and full of many possibilities which will not be determined until human free choices have been made.

The problem with this attractive view is that God's knowledge becomes really restricted. God would not have known in the 1950s that Eastern Europe would move away from Communism; God would not have known in 1999 of the horrors awaiting human beings in the new millennium. Such limitation on God may be unacceptable.

2 *Freedom to act according to our nature*: If freedom is the freedom to act according to our nature (termed 'liberty of spontaneity'), then human beings are free to do whatever they wish to do, but what they wish to do is determined by their nature, background and education. Luke would be free to marry Petunia since this would be what Luke wanted to do, but his wishes would be wholly determined by his education, social conditioning and genetics.

If people were hypnotised they would still, on this view, be regarded as having freedom to act according to their nature as they would be acting as they would want to. However, these wants would be determined by the hypnotist. Similarly, it is held, we may have the freedom to act in accordance with our nature but our nature may be wholly determined. This view of human freedom may therefore be compatible with predestination by God. We would think we are free, but we would lack the freedom to choose between alternatives as we are determined by our genetics or by the society in which we live.

If we have this form of freedom – and there is no way, in principle, of proving which type of freedom we have – then the everlasting God could know, in the present, our future free actions, since these actions would be wholly determined by our nature.

Most theologians and philosophers want to maintain that we have genuine freedom (the first of the above alternatives). If, therefore, they work with a model of God as everlasting they are willing to restrict God's knowledge of the future, so far as this future is affected by the free actions of human beings. Peter Geach produced a helpful way of looking at God's knowledge of our future free actions. Geach likens God to a Grand Chessmaster. If we were playing chess with a grand master, we would be completely free to make any move on the board. There would be no external constraint on us, but there would also be no doubt that we would lose. Geach puts it this way:

> God is the supreme Grand Master who has everything under his control. Some of the prayers are consciously helping his plan, others are trying to hinder it; whatever the finite players do, God's plan will be executed; though various lines of God's play will answer to various moves of the finite players. God cannot be surprised or thwarted or cheated or disappointed. God, like some Grand Master at chess, can carry out his plan even if he has announced it beforehand. 'On that square,' says the Grand Master, 'I will promote my pawn to Queen and deliver check-mate to my adversary,' and it is even so (*Providence and Evil*, Cambridge, 1977, p. 58).

The idea of God as a Grand Master is, in my view, helpful, but not in the way Geach presents it. On his view, the Grand Master can, somehow, predict every move the finite opponents will make, and this interferes with human freedom. Even I, a very weak chess player, could prevent a grand master from 'promoting his pawn to Queen and delivering checkmate' if he were to announce his plan in advance.

However, Geach's image of the Grand Master can be adapted. Agreed, a grand chessmaster will beat us. So, it may be held, it is with God. The everlasting God knows all the future possibilities that are open to us, even though God does not know specifically which choices we will make. However, because God is God and we are mere humans, we cannot frustrate God's long-term purposes and intentions, in other words, we cannot thwart God's plans. So I would argue that the everlasting God cannot predict with absolute certainty our every future action. However, God can know that God's eventual purposes will triumph, just as the grand master can predict that he will win the game.

The everlasting God could, therefore, leave human beings free to make any choices they wish, within the limitations imposed by their humanity. We can do as we wish, and God may well leave us free to make choices for ourselves about the sort of individuals we shall become. We are free to decide whether we shall become people capable of love and self-sacrifice or whether we will allow the demands of self to take pride of place and thus become cold and indifferent to others. We can choose, and we must take the consequences of our choices. However, God's wider purposes cannot be thwarted. God can, for example, ensure that we do not drag others down with us (for instance by providing help from others to counteract what we choose to do). We cannot defeat God but we can nevertheless choose our own paths.

Exactly what God's purposes are we may not know, but the picture remains an attractive one. It emphasizes God's personality and does not allow God's lack of knowledge about our future free actions to take the world out of God's control. God interacts with the world. Thus in the Hebrew Scriptures, God has to act time after time to bring God's chosen people back to obedience. God's ultimate act was the sending of God's Son, out of love for men and women, to bring people to see the mistakes they were making in their lives. However, even this act was ambiguous – people were left free to ignore it if they wished, and those who shouted 'Hosanna!' on Palm Sunday were shouting 'Crucify him!' a few days later. God could do nothing about this without destroying human freedom, and if this freedom were taken away, so would be any possibility of people being brought to love God.

The view of God as everlasting – with God's omniscience restricted to knowledge of past and present truths as well as future true statements that are directly due to present events (for instance, the future state of the physical universe) – emphasises the personality of God and is easy to understand. God knows all future possibilities. God knew the possibility of Auschwitz and Stalin's death camps, but could not have prevented these without destroying human freedom. God does, the believer maintains, act in the world to ensure that God's long-term intentions are brought about. The disadvantage is that God has to act in the universe to ensure that the free actions of men and women do not undermine God's purposes, and some may hold that this is too anthropomorphic a view of God.

Believers in an everlasting God will be anti-realists about future statements in so far as these statements refer to the future actions of human beings. They will thus deny that there is any truth to be known until the actions take place.

The anti-realist view of God

The two views of omniscience considered so far involve a God who created the universe and who knows past and present facts. The wholly simple, timeless God knows future facts, whereas the everlasting God's knowledge of the future is more problematic. If, however, we adopt an anti-realist understanding of language about God, than there is no God who can know in any conventional sense. What, then, are we going to make of talk of omniscience? On the anti-realist view, religious language tells us something about the human condition. It shows us something about what it means for human beings to live in the world. Talk of omniscience is talk about our inability to evade the reality against which our lives must be measured. We know ourselves and we cannot escape from our own judgement of ourselves.

In Robert Bolt's play *A Man for All Seasons*, Thomas More, the Lord Chancellor of England, tells the young ambitious courtier, Rich, who has come to him seeking advancement at court, that his intended ambitions are mistaken. More advises Rich to become a teacher. If he is a good teacher, More says, 'You will know it, your pupils will know it and God will know it.' Stewart Sutherland (in *God, Jesus and Belief*, Blackwell, 1984) claims that in saying 'God will know it,' More need not be referring to a CIA, a Celestial Intelligence Agency, which monitors the movements of every human being and which will judge and condemn every word or action that is spoken against the will of the power-figure who controls the universe. Such an understanding is too crude.

Instead, to talk of God's omniscience is to show that the different way of living life that is possible cannot be evaded or avoided. The possibility of the life of holiness and self-giving love is available for us to follow or to reject. We cannot, however, hide our doings in secret, since the actions we take make us the sort of people we become. It is this that will decide whether or not we can overcome the trivialisation that death and old age can easily bring.

Aristotle said that, at first, an individual has the power to choose the path of vice or virtue. However, as our lives continue, so the path we have chosen becomes easier and easier. We become set in our ways, and virtue or vice eventually has power over us. We have made ourselves individuals of a certain type. Our sinful doings, on this view, are not things that we vainly try to hide from an omniscient being. Instead, talk of omniscience reminds us that nothing is hidden, since all our hidden sins determine what sort of people we become. We cannot easily escape their effects, nor can we escape our own knowledge of what we have done. Our sins will find us out.

Summary

The wholly simple, timeless God has all time simultaneously present to God, so that events which, to us, are past, present and future are all alike to Him. If God's knowledge causes our actions then we are determined and not free but if God's knowledge depends on our actions then there are real questions whether God can still be held to be simple.

The everlasting God knows the past and the present. Such a God can know the future only insofar as it is determined by the way things are in the universe now. If, therefore, human beings only have the freedom to act in accordance with their determined nature then it would be possible for the everlasting God to know the future.

If, however, human beings have genuine freedom to choose between alternatives, then the everlasting God cannot know the future insofar as it could be affected by the free choices of human beings. Such a God could still be held to be omniscient, as God would know all that it is logically possible to know.

If we instead adopt a revisionary account to explain theological language, then talk about omniscience is a way of showing that we cannot escape the effects of our actions. We become the sort of people our acts make us and, in this sense, all that is hidden will be revealed.

Questions for consideration

a) If God knows that you will have cornflakes for breakfast tomorrow, are you free to have toast instead?
b) Is our future, future to God?
c) How might you argue that you are completely determined and yet free?
d) If there is no creator God, in what way might it make sense for a believer to talk of God being omniscient?
e) If God is timeless, why might one want to hold that God's knowledge causes events to happen?

SECTION 5

GOD'S ACTION

FIFTEEN

Petitionary Prayer

There are many different types of prayer and it becomes more difficult to talk philosophically when one gets to the heart of prayer. There is a danger of philosophers 'doing violence' (as Wittgenstein termed it) to what religious believers understand prayer to be. Prayer is a sign of a believer's relationship to God and represents a conscious turning towards God. Philosophers have long recognised the importance of petitionary prayer. In the *Timaeus*, Socrates insists that the gods should be called upon before any serious scientific enquiry is undertaken and similarly Critias acknowledges that no sensible person would fail to call upon God before beginning any serious undertaking. The main philosophic problems occur in relation to petitionary prayer – in other words, when asking for God to do something.

At the time of the wedding of Prince Charles and Diana, the Dean of St. Paul's appeared on national television and said: 'Pray for the young couple. You know it makes a difference.' The question is what kind of difference it makes. Jesus said that 'The Father will give you whatever you ask in my name' (John 15:16), yet even when apparently worthy things are asked for such as peace or relief from suffering many prayers are not answered. Eleanore Stump says that 'If there were a point to petitionary prayer, the insurance companies would be the first to know it since the death rate for people prayed for would be lower than people not prayed for' (*A Companion to Philosophy of Religion*, edited by P. Quinn and C. Taliaferno, Blackwell, 1977, p. 580).

There are three main alternatives:

1 Petitionary prayer is asking God, regarded as either (a) a wholly simple, timeless substance, or (b) as an everlasting Spirit, to act in order to bring about some change in the spatio-temporal world as a result of the prayer:

2 Petitionary prayer involves changes in the believer or the community of which the person making the prayer is a part, or

3 Petitionary prayer builds a relationship with God.

One of these does not rule out the other, but if petitionary prayer is seen at least partly as involving (1), then the philosophic problems increase. We will take these alternatives in turn.

Petitionary prayer as asking God to bring about some change in the world

Many believers regard prayer as making requests to God, which they hope God may grant by acting in the world. They would see the world being different because God can and sometimes does act in the world in response to prayer. However there are considerable difficulties with this idea.

Aquinas, prayer and freedom

Aquinas argues that the wholly simple God's action can either be direct, a primary action, or action through human beings under the principle of *Double Agency*. Double agency maintains that God can act through people: individuals can act but God also acts through them, so there can be a double agency: the agency (or action) of both the individual or group and of God. Both agents are present in the one action. God can, therefore, be seen as acting through people. A dramatic example of this was when the prophet Jeremiah told the Israelites that God was going to send them into exile, and that God was going to use the Babylonians as the agent to punish them for their disobedience. The Babylonians would defeat them in war and the walls of Jerusalem would be torn down. Although the agent who was to carry out the destruction was the Babylonian army, Jeremiah says that God is acting through them. God's hand, therefore, is seen in history and in individual human actions.

Aquinas maintains that God timelessly knows what all believers pray. He says:

> We must pray, not to inform God of our needs and desires but in order to remind ourselves that in these matters we need divine assistance (*Summa Theologiae* 2a, 2ae, 83).

> We do not pray in order to change the decrees of Divine providence, rather we pray in order to acquire by petitionary prayer what God has determined will be obtained by our prayers.

> Everything God wills comes about (*Summa Theologiae* 1a, 19, 8).

Aquinas has difficulty in explaining unanswered prayer and he does not really address the problem. However, there is a much graver difficulty that has been discussed in the chapter on Omniscience, namely that Aquinas considers God's knowledge to be causal (notice the words 'has determined' in the above quotation). In other words, Aquinas considers that it is God's will that is the source of God's knowledge and it is God's knowledge of events that causes these events to occur. Aquinas has no idea of human beings being free as against God. Aquinas needs to maintain that God's will is causal in order to ensure that God is not affected by the created order and that God's knowledge is identical to all God's other attributes. This position has to be maintained in order to hold fast to the simplicity of God, the core of the idea of God stemming from traditional Roman Catholic theology. However, as has been made clear in the earlier chapter, this position leads to determinism as it is God's knowledge that a person prays that causes the person to pray.

As we have seen, Fr. Gerry Hughes (in *The Nature of God*) recognises this in his chapter on omniscience and concludes that Aquinas' position must be rejected. Hughes maintains that it is the free action of human beings that causes God's knowledge.

It is not clear, however, that a *de re* necessary God, all of whose attributes are identical to each other, can depend for God's knowledge on the contingent actions of human beings (see p. 161). In other words, if

1 God knows events in the created universe including the free, contingent, actions of human beings (such as human beings freely deciding to pray), and

2 It is these free actions (e.g. the person deciding to pray) that cause God's knowledge, this may mean that

3 God's knowledge must also be contingent as it is dependent on contingent events.

This problem is of great importance if one works with a wholly simple, timeless God. If Aquinas' position is maintained, then prayer becomes determined and human freedom is eliminated, clearly a position most believers would regard as unsatisfactory. If this is the case, then petitionary prayer cannot be seen as asking God to respond to our requests.

There seem, therefore, to be two alternatives:

1 To maintain that God's knowledge is causal and that God therefore causes human beings to do everything they do (including prayer) in which case human beings are determined, or

2 To maintain that God depends on human beings' prayer for God's knowledge that they will pray. In this case God's simplicity may be undermined and this may mean that God has to be in time rather than timeless. Gerry Hughes maintains that God can depend for his knowledge on human beings and still be wholly simple. I am not at all sure this is possible, though!

This is a crucial issue if one wishes to hold that God is wholly simple and timeless as it may mean that human beings cannot be free to pray.

Which prayers are answered?

If one maintains that there is a creator God (either an everlasting, suffering God or, if the problem in the previous section can be overcome, a wholly simple, timeless God) who can and does act in the world in response to prayer, it is very difficult to know which events are answers to prayers and which would have happened in any case. There can be a tendency to attribute to God those things that happened as they were prayed for, and to explain those that did not happen as they were prayed for, either to a 'no' response from God or to other factors such as lack of faith by the person praying. However, if God only intervenes in answer to prayer 'sometimes', what criteria might be used to decide which are the 'sometimes'? Assume that a mother has lost her husband and has no money. Her children are cold and hungry. She prays to God for help and the next day an unknown uncle dies and leaves her a substantial legacy. Should this be seen as an action of God? Similarly, if someone recovers from illness after prayer, why attribute this to God rather than simply to the skill of the doctors? If it is held that God works 'through' the doctors, then this has to be analysed and explained: what, precisely, does it mean? What is the difference between

1 'The doctor cured his son,' and
2 'God, working through the doctor's skill, cured his son'?

Perhaps, it may be argued, the only difference is in the eye of the believer. If this is the case, then this can make answered prayer close to being whatever a believer considers to be answered prayer, which is not a very helpful definition. This would come close to the anti-realist position dealt with below: within the form of life of the believing community beneficial events that turn out as they were prayed for will be spoken of in terms of 'answered prayer'. Outside the believing community, to non-believers, this language will not be used. There is also the problem that, if God is seen as permanently active in all aspects of the life of the universe, how can God then be seen as more active in response to prayer than at other times? This raises the whole issue of unanswered prayer and why so many prayers for apparently worthy causes are not answered. If it is held that God does answer some prayers and not others, then this can be questioned by asking why prayer should be relevant at all. God is held to be omniscient, omnipotent and wholly good: God knows the needs of people without their asking and would bring about the best state of affairs independently of whether a person is prayed for. As Helen Oppenheimer puts it: 'What is hard to believe in is a God who is supposed to withhold his favour from some apparently worthy person or cause for whom no one has happened to pray.'

Stump recognises that petitionary prayer seems incongruent since 'the recipient of the prayer is supposed to be omniscient, omnipotent, perfectly good and possessed of the other standard divine attributes' (*A Companion to Philosophy of Religion*, edited by P. Quinn and C. Taliaferno, Blackwell, 1977, ch. 73.) Throughout the world, people pray to God yet their prayers appear to be unanswered. One might assume, however, that this would lead them to lose faith in God, but in fact this is not the case. It is clear that although many believers do pray to God and do trust that God can answer their prayers, they also accept that many prayers will not be answered and this in no way undermines their faith.

The understanding of petitionary prayer one adopts is going to be directly influenced by one's understanding of what sort of God one believes in and how this God relates to creation. The question, therefore, of the difference that prayer is held to make is central to one's understanding of the nature of God.

The problem of selective activity by God
Even if God can act in the world and even if there is some basis for deciding which events are due to answered prayer and which are not, an even more serious challenge remains to the idea of petitionary

prayer as asking God to act in the world.

Maurice Wiles (in *God's Action in the World*, SCM Press, 1986) rejects the idea of any interventions by God into the created universe. Wiles argues that the universe is part of a single, ongoing act of creation by God but denies God the ability to intervene specifically in the world. This is because, if God could do so, God would not be worthy of worship. If God could act to cure a child at Lourdes or to make statues weep or the blood of saints not to clot or to help some individual in relatively trivial ways, then this would, Wiles maintains, mean that God would not be worthy of worship as if God *could* intervene and failed to do so in cases like Stalin's death camps, the Rwanda and Kosovo massacres, the Bosnian conflicts, earthquakes, etc. God would have to be rejected as not being worthy of worship. Wiles rejects all special interventions by God and maintains that even paradigm interventions like the incarnation or resurrection of Jesus have to be understood in alternative ways than in terms of selective divine action. It is important to separate Wiles' position from that of Phillips set out below. Wiles is a realist – he maintains that there is a creator God. However, Wiles considers that this God only performs a single act, which is to create and sustain the universe.

Keith Ward in *Divine Action* (Collins, Flame, 1990) attempts to address the challenge laid down by Wiles. Ward maintains God can and does act in response to prayer, but is restricted in any ability to intervene. God would only act for the best, but sometimes there is no single best possible action available. Ward goes on:

If the Divine plan is to a large extent open, he may consent to realize a certain state just because it is requested (ibid., p. 159).

Our request may make it possible for [God] to help ... in ways which would otherwise have been constrained by the structures of the natural order (ibid., p. 166).

Ward claims when Jesus says, 'If two of you on earth agree about anything you ask for, it will be done for you by my father in heaven' (Matthew 18:19) this is 'poetic hyperbole, so typical of the teaching of Jesus' (ibid., p. 166).

Ward maintains that there are three constraints on God's ability to answer prayer:

1 Prayer must arise in the context of worship, or a relationship of loving obedience to God. It is no use disobeying God in most things and asking for God's help when it suits us. Christians, Ward says, pray 'through Jesus Christ' and in so doing name their ultimate object of loyalty.

2 Prayers must be for the good of others and must be supported by loving action whenever possible. The believer must leave God to judge whether something that is prayed for is truly for the good of others or not.

3 Prayers must be for what is possible. Ward says: 'I have suggested that what is possible for God, within the structures he has created, will depend on factors of probability, system-stability and alternative causal pathways, which cannot in principle be known to us.' (p. 167)

So God *can* answer prayers, but his ability to do so is much constrained. A story from Ray Bradbury illustrates this. A package holiday company in the year 2050 sends tourists back in time to shoot dinosaurs, but they are subject to very strict rules that they may not leave laid-down paths or damage anything other than the selected target. The tour operator explains:

If you step on a mouse, you kill families of mice – a thousand, a million, a billion mice annihilated. For want of ten mice a fox dies, for want of ten foxes a lion starves, for want of a lion, all sorts of insects, vultures, infinite billions of life forms are thrown into chaos and destruction. Eventually, 59 million years later a caveman, one of a dozen in the entire world, goes hunting wild boar or sabre-toothed tiger for food. But you, friend, have stepped on all the tigers in that region – by stepping on a single mouse. So the caveman starves. And the caveman, note, is not just any expendable man. No! He is an entire future nature. Destroy this one man, and you destroy a race, a people, an entire history of life (Ray Bradbury, 'A Sound of Thunder', in *Collected Short Stories*).

Tiny actions by God could have incalculable effects. Assume a young woman thinks she is pregnant and prays to God that this should not be true. If God acted to bring it about that she was no longer pregnant, then the whole history of the world changes. Because she does not have a child, her life, her partner's life and her family's life will be changed forever. If she had had the child it would have grown up and mixed with others – their lives would all have been affected. The child would have had relationships of his or her own and so the ripples would have extended down the ages. Any action by God has the most enormous effects and it simply is not possible for God to intervene continually. God's ability to act is, therefore, greatly restricted. One problem with Ward's view is that it may place too great a limitation on God and might reinforce the idea of God as no more than a cosmic superhuman figure and this might be considered religiously inadequate.

It is true that some Christian and all Islamic theology sees all events as happening 'according to the will of Allah' but if everything happens by God's will this raises intractable problems with human free will. If, as an alternative, selective action is allowed it is precisely the selectivity by God that raises the problem.

Petitionary prayer as bringing about changes in the believer

In the first understanding of petitionary prayer set out above, such prayer was regarded as asking for God to make changes in the world. However, petitionary prayer does not have to be seen like this. Instead, the emphasis may be switched to seeing such prayer as primarily involving changes in the person who prays. Such an understanding is usually taken by those who advocate a non-realist understanding of God.

If the word 'God' does not refer to a creator God who acts in the world, an account of petitionary prayer is needed that does not involve asking a creator God to act. The very idea of prayer as asking an agent called God to act can be seen as fundamentally flawed. In his book *The Concept of Prayer* (Blackwell, 1981), D. Z. Phillips has produced an excellent account of prayer which, he claims, avoids the problem of prayer becoming something like superstition. Phillips says that it is important to distinguish petitionary prayer from magic. It makes sense in magic to say 'She did not have the right spell' (e.g. not enough frog's legs or newts' eyes in the cauldron). Can we similarly say:

1 'Her prayers were not answered because she was not a good Christian or did not have enough faith'?

2 'She did not pray hard enough'?

Phillips attempts to give an account of petitionary prayer that does not relapse into superstition and he considers it superstitious to suppose that petitionary prayer is actually asking God to act. He contrasts talking to a person and talking to God. In particular, he claims that prayer is only genuine when part of a way of life devoted to God. He gives two examples of what he considers to be non-genuine prayers as they are words spoken in a moment of crisis with no religious significance:

> Bonhoeffer gives an example of this in telling of an incident during a heavy bombing raid on a concentration camp where he was a prisoner. 'As we were all lying on the floor yesterday, someone muttered "O God, O God" – he is normally a frivolous sort of chap – but I couldn't bring myself to offer him any Christian encouragement or comfort. All I did was to glance at

my watch and say: 'It won't last any more than ten minutes now' (*Letters and Papers from Prison*, p. 67).

One leg was gone and the other was held by tendons and part of the trouser and the stump twitched and jerked as though it were not connected. He bit his arm and moaned 'Oh, mamma mia, mamma mia', then 'Dio ti salvi, Maria. Dio ti salvi Maria. O Jesus shoot me, Christ shoot me. Mamma mia, mamma mia of purest lovely Mary shoot me. Stop it. Stop it. Stop it. Oh lovely Jesus lovely Mary stop it. Oh, oh, oh' then choking 'Mamma mamma mia' (in *A Farewell to Arms*, p. 47, quoted in *The Concept of Prayer*, p. 116).

Phillips' position that genuine prayer can take place only as part of a life devoted to God may be challenged. Perhaps in moments of real crisis genuine prayers by people who are not normally committed to a religious way of life may be possible, although in the two fairly extreme examples above it seems that Phillips does indeed have a point.

Prayer, for Phillips, is not a substitute for effort. It is no good praying for someone in need when you are in a position to help and do nothing. To pass by the beggar on the street and to pray for him when you have money in your pocket and are not willing to help, could scarcely be regarded as genuine prayer. Prayer is a ritual whose point lies in itself. There is no external point in terms of some result to be achieved. Prayer that is only considered worthwhile if some end is achieved in terms of an intervention is, says Phillips, superstitious. When a believer prays, she goes apart from the world to reorder priorities and possible future actions. The pious form of petitionary prayer is 'Thy will be done' and the prayer will be answered no matter what happens. Prayer is a means of finding meaning and hope whatever the outcome may be. Phillips says: 'The love of God's will can be found in whatever happens, but the prayer of petition is best understood, not as an attempt at influencing the way things go, but as an expression of, and a request for, devotion to God through the way things go' (ibid., p. 120).

Phillips quotes the examples of

- A boxer who crosses himself before a fight, and
- A mother with a sick child who lights a candle in front of a statue of the Virgin Mary

In both cases the individuals, Phillips claims, are trying to find a way to live through whatever happens. Whatever the result of the fight the boxer is seeking the strength to live with success or failure. In the case of the mother, if the child recovers he is received back as a renewed gift whilst if he dies the mother finds meaning and the strength to get through when she never thought she could get through. Fr. Gareth Moore in his book *Believing in God, a Philosophical Essay* in the chapter on Prayer argues that to say 'God helped me to get through' is to say that nothing helped you to get through – you got through when you never thought you would be able to get through. You found the strength to cope when you were sure there was no hope of finding the strength. Moore says:

> what answers my prayer is not that I get what I asked for and that a particular agent, viz. God, does something that constitutes his giving it to me. What answers my prayer is simply that I get what I want. The question of agency does not arise ... What I pray for when I pray for something is not that a particular agent do something with the intention and result that I receive something; I pray simply to receive it. It is not that I want somebody to do something, but that I want something to happen (*Believing in God, a Philosophical Essay*, T. & T. Clarke, 1988, p. 207).

For Moore, God is nothing, God is not an agent who acts. If a prayer is answered it simply means that what has been prayed for has happened. It is important that Moore does not consider that God was simply 'no-thing' as Aquinas would do. He goes much further and considers that God is nothing. When one prays to God one does not pray to anything. This is very close, if not identical, to the anti-realist view and, therefore, Moore rejects all ideas of prayer having anything to do with asking God to act in the world.

Phillips contrasts a diver 'praying' in a moment of crisis and true prayer:

> I heard a diver tell of an experience which occurred while he was searching a wreck. He lost his torch and could not find the exit to the hold. He prayed 'O God get me out of this. I'll do anything you want if only you'll let me find my way out'. Compare that prayer with 'Yea, though I walk through the valley of the shadow of death I will fear no evil, for thou art with me' (Psalm 23).

Here is a summary of Phillips' account of prayer:

1 Prayer to God requires genuine devotion. We can decide whether prayer is genuine by looking at the role it has in an individual's life.

2 Prayer involves coming to self-knowledge, meditation on one's wants and 'bringing them before God'. In prayer, the believer is recognising his or her wants before the existing reality that is God. (We must remember that for Phillips God certainly exists – but not as a creator who is apart from the universe that God has created. God exists as a reality within the form of life of the believing community. To say that Phillips does not believe in God is seriously to misunderstand the anti-realist position.)

3 Prayer is a way of finding meaning and hope in life whatever happens.

4. Wittgenstein gives an example of the tribe that prays for rain every year at the time when it is due to rain in any case. It might be claimed that this is similar to the Church of England's Rogation and Harvest Thanksgiving services. The Rogation service takes place in the spring and asks for God's blessing on the crops, whilst at the Harvest

Thanksgiving (one of the very best attended of the Church of England's services in the year) believers give thanks for the harvest. However bad or good the harvest, believers still give thanks.

Phillips claims that Wittgenstein's example of the tribe praying for rain is intended to show that there is no objective point to the ritual dance – the prayer takes place when the rain is due in any case. Instead, there is a subjective point. The prayer is expressive. The believer is expressing feelings of dependence and is recognising his or her part in the totality of the earth. The believer is definitely *not* asking for God to intervene in some way to change the weather.

When the Catholic goes to Mass, when the Muslim prays five times a day, when the Jew goes to the synagogue, he or she is recognising his or her finitude and getting away from the world so as to reorder his or her priorities.

5. The pious form of petitionary prayer is 'Thy will be done.' This is the key to all such prayer. Petitionary prayer is answered no matter what happens.

6. Prayer is not a substitute for effort. One cannot pray and then sit back in the hope that God will do the necessary work. Instead, prayer is a means of accepting whatever will be the case. *It is a ritual the point of which lies in itself.*

7. Petitionary prayer thus brings about a change in the believer. Through prayer the individual comes to recognise that some desires are not those of God. the whole of life can thereby come to be seen in a new way.

Phillips' point is that prayer in no sense depends on, nor does it seek, any particular outcome. As he says: 'When deep believers pray *for* something, they are not so much asking God to bring it about, but in a way telling him of the strength of their desires.' Phillips (and Gareth Moore) are, essentially, anti-realists and, although they deny this, their accounts of petitionary prayer *are* revisionary. Most ordinary believers believe that prayer *does*, in some sense, involve addressing a being or Spirit called God and that there is at least the possibility of these prayers being answered. Although Phillips says that this is superstitious, Jesus himself seems to have been superstitious in that his prayers were addressed to his Father and seemed to expect a response. Phillips is not, therefore, faithful to Wittgenstein (to whom he constantly appeals) as Wittgenstein said that philosophy should 'leave everything as it is' – Phillips lays down what the believer's prayer should be and how it should be understood, and in so doing he distorts what many believers themselves maintain that they are doing.

It is worth being clear here that this understanding of prayer is not only held by anti-realists. If one believes in a creator God who created the universe and sustains it, it is quite possible to believe that God nevertheless does not respond to prayer. In fact, this was the position of Maurice Wiles set out earlier in this chapter. In this case, one could be a realist and still maintain this understanding of petitionary prayer.

Petitionary prayer as developing a relationship with God

The first of the three alternative ways of understanding petitionary prayer sees this prayer as asking God to bring about changes in the world which would not have happened except for this prayer. The second understanding concentrates on the believer seeing petitionary prayer as effectively praying 'thy will be done' and coming to accept whatever happens. There is, however, a third understanding which sees *all* prayer, including petitionary prayer, as primarily involving building a relationship between the believer and God.

Vincent Brummer in his *What Are We Doing When We Pray?* (SPCK, 1984) does accept that prayer is asking for God to act, but he mainly focuses on such prayer being seen as part of developing a relationship with God. Without our requests, God can bring about what we need, but he cannot *give* us anything. Prayer is, therefore, a matter of opening ourselves to what God is going to give and coming to see it is a gift rather than as a brute fact of nature.

God sends the rain to the just and the unjust; but to the just who has asked for it, it comes as a token of God's goodness, whereas to the unjust who never says 'Please' and never says 'thank you', it is a mere climatic condition, without significance and without being an occasion for gratitude; and the unjusts' life is thereby poorer and drearier.

Brummer does want to say that God is also influenced by prayer, although his argument is not always readily apparent as to how this operates. He recognises that there is a two-way contingency involved in requests to God. In other words, it is neither inevitable nor impossible that God should answer prayers. He clearly works with an everlasting model of God who is capable of change whilst being unchanging in terms of God's character.

Brummer maintains that the purpose of petitionary prayer is to recognise one's duties and responsibilities, to pray for others, to dedicate oneself to God and to open oneself to God's will. In prayer believers acknowledge their dependency and make themselves available as collaborators in God's purposes. For Brummer, God acts through human beings who open themselves for God to act through them. God enables and motivates people to do his will *provided* they choose to be open to him. Brummer accepts that this view implies a God who is not in total control of the universe.

One problem with Brummer's approach is that it is not entirely clear how it differs from that of the anti-realist. According to Brummer, much depends on the way the world is seen by the believer (as gift rather than brute fact) and it is not entirely clear what space, if any, he allows for direct action by God.

In spite of the possible shortcomings with Brummer's analysis, it does have the advantage of stressing prayer as building a relationship. Just as in any other relationship one may express one's wishes and hopes as part of the openness that lies between two people who love each other. In this sense, praying to God is seen as rather similar to talking to another person. But the main focus of the prayer is to develop the relationship with God rather than, specifically, to hope that God will act in response to prayer. Such an understanding may, indeed, be close to what many believers consider to be happening in prayer, but it must be recognised that it is somewhat vague on whether prayer as building relationship does or does not envisage that God can and will act in response to requests made in prayer. It is here, as we have seen earlier in this chapter, that the philosophic difficulties arise.

Summary

The understanding one has of petitionary prayer will largely depend on the model of God with which one is operating. In all views of God, petitionary prayer will be seen as meditative, as having therapeutic value and as bringing about changes in the believer and in members of his or her community. In the anti–realist revisionary accounts of language about God (in other words, where God is a reality within the form of life of the believing community or where talk about God is talk about a possible way of living life), this will be all that petitionary prayer involves. 'Thy will be done' will be the heart of all prayer.

If God is a wholly simple, timeless substance or an everlasting Spirit, then prayer can form part of a two-way, I/Thou relationship with God in which the believer makes requests which God may or may not answer. There is a problem if God is wholly simple and God's will causes us to pray, as then human beings are not free.

If prayer is considered to be asking God to act, then the challenge of Wiles needs to be faced, namely that there are considerable philosophic difficulties with the idea of a God who can act in the world and who chooses to do so in such a selective fashion, ignoring requests which we, as human beings, would not fail to respond to if we had the power to do so. Some believers will be happy to ignore this, either trusting in God's wisdom or maintaining, with Ward, that God's ability to act is greatly constrained by the world that God has created. In no case are there clear criteria for determining on what basis God acts in reply to prayer. All forms of prayer may be seen as developing a relationship between the believer and God, although precisely what this involves is not always easy to define.

Questions for consideration

a) If a believer prays for a child who is dying of throat cancer, what is she doing?

b) If there is a God who sometimes acts in response to prayer, could such selective action ever be morally justifiable?

c) 'Ask and it shall be given to you, seek and you shall find, knock and it shall be opened unto you.' What do you think this means?

d) 'All petitionary prayer is asking "They will be done."' Is this an adequate analysis of petitionary prayer?

e) What is 'double agency'?

f) How is talking to God different from talking to a friend?

SIXTEEN

Praying for Forgiveness

Every Christian, Muslim or Jew who takes part in any form of worship prays for forgiveness. Almost without exception services include confession of sin. In some churches, there are not only *general confessions* (confessions of sin made by the whole congregation using a set form of words) but also *personal confessions* in which an individual either goes to a priest to confess his or her sins and to be absolved from them, or else confesses his or sins to the community of which he or she forms a part. A typical general confession is that used by the Church of England in its Alternative Service Book 1980:

> Almighty God, our heavenly Father,
> We have sinned against you and against our fellow men,
> in thought and word and deed
> through negligence, through weakness,
> through our own deliberate fault.
> We are truly sorry
> and repent of all our sins.
> For the sake of your Son Jesus Christ, who died for us,
> forgive us all that is past;
> and grant that we may serve you in newness of life
> to the glory of your name. Amen.

The question we need to ask is what the believer thinks is happening when he or she prays for forgiveness. One question that obviously arises here is what is mean by sin. There can be many different approaches. Sin may be seen as (i) breaking rules, such as the Ten Commandments; (ii) acting against the law of love; (iii) turning away from God; or (iv) ceasing to live up to our true human nature. We shall not be discussing the different approaches to sin because, whatever view is taken, praying for forgiveness involves seeking to deal with the situation that the believer's sins have created. Certainly, praying for forgiveness involves repentance, and this must be genuine. Sorrow for sins committed is an essential part of any genuine prayer for forgiveness.

The different possibilities can well be illustrated by a series of diagrams involving the following four possible parties:

The individual

It is true that in some churches prayers for forgiveness do not ask for forgiveness of an individual but rather for forgiveness of a group of people. You will notice that the prayer above said, 'We have sinned against you and against our fellow men.' However, any community is made up of individuals – it is not the community that is guilty so much as all those who make up the community. They share, in different ways, in the guilt. Sin is an individual business, although it is true that some sins can result from sharing in evil structures. It might, for instance, be held that the affluent, materialistic and selfish lifestyle of the Western world is sinful because millions are starving in the Third World. However, this corporate sin cannot remove responsibility from each of us, as individuals, for our part in that sin. This point is made by Rudyard Kipling's poem 'Tomlinson', about a man of that name who dies and comes before St Peter at Heaven's entrance gate. St Peter says:

> 'Stand up, stand up now, Tomlinson, and answer loud and high
> The good that ye did for the sake of men or ever ye came to die –
> The good that ye did for the sake of men on little earth so lone!'
> And the naked soul of Tomlinson grew white as a rain-washed bone.
> 'Oh, I have a friend on earth,' he said, 'that was my priest and guide,
> And well would he answer all for me if he were at my side.'

'For that ye strove in neighbour-love it shall be written fair,
But now ye wait at Heaven's Gate and not in Berkeley Square:
Though we called your friend from his bed this night, he could not
* speak for you,*
For the race is run by one and one and never by two and two.'
Then Tomlinson looked up and down, and little gain was there
For the naked stars grinned overhead, and he saw that his soul was
* bare ...*

Christianity, Islam and Judaism have all affirmed in their different ways that 'the race is run by one and one and never by two and two'. Further on in the poem Tomlinson comes face to face with the Devil, and the same point is made again: 'For the sin ye do by two and two, ye must pay for one by one.' In other words, we must take responsibility for our own actions. We cannot hide behind membership of a community in order to disclaim individual responsibility.

Praying for forgiveness is something that each individual must do – whether together with or apart from others. Individuality cannot be subsumed under any broader category. It is we as individuals who act, we who live our lives and we who must take the consequences of the choices we make.

The priest

In some churches priests are not particularly important theologically – at least in terms of any hierarchial status. They are not any different from the ordinary members of the congregation, even though they may be leaders of their community. This might apply, for instance, in the Baptist, Methodist, Pentecostal or Reformed churches. In the Catholic,   Orthodox   and   Anglican   churches   on the other hand, the priest is a theologically pivotal figure, able to pronounce forgiveness of sins in a way that no layperson can do. The different models below, therefore, sometimes incorporate the priest and sometimes do not.

The community

The Catholic Church, in particular, stresses the importance of community. Indeed 'community' has become a key phrase amongst Catholics since the Second Vatican Council, and it is difficult to find a Catholic pronouncement that does not feature the word. To be a Catholic is, to a very real extent, to belong to the Catholic community. All churches have some sense of community, and in praying for forgiveness one of the things the believer may be doing is becoming reconciled to his or her community, because he or she has sinned against it.

God

We need two views of God in order to take account of the two main possibilities:

1 *The creator God*: This is the wholly simple, timeless God or the everlasting, suffering God who is an agent who created the universe. In prayer for forgiveness this God may well be involved and can respond to that prayer. It makes sense to talk of a two-way relationship with this God.

2 *God*: This is the anti-realist view of God. God is not in any sense an agent; God did not create the universe. God does, indeed, exist and is a reality within the form of life of the believing community. God may well be essential as a focus for the believers' prayers, but God does not and cannot respond, as this God is not in any sense a being or spirit that could respond.

With these basic categories established, we can now move on to look at the different interpretations of what it means to pray for forgiveness.

Model 1.

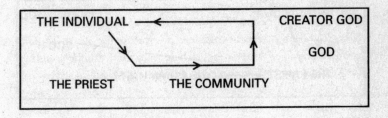

John prays for forgiveness and meditates about his life. He thinks about how he has failed to follow the path of love, how he has been unkind to his parents, how he has lied to his sister and how he has been selfish. He thinks about the hurt he has caused and is genuinely sorry. He resolves to try very hard to mend his ways and to be the kind and loving person he would really like to be in the future. Having recognised his sins, he goes on his way refreshed. He knows where he is and is resolved to do better in the future.

On this model, praying for forgiveness involves John in coming to self-knowledge. When he prays, he measures his life against his ideal and recognises his failings. He sees himself as he really is and resolves to become a better person. He is thus able to live with himself.

In Dostoevsky's *The Brothers Karamazov*, a man confesses to a priest the murder he committed 15 years previously. Because of the confession, the man is able to come to terms with what he has done and to find the strength to continue his life, freed from the chains of his past sin. However, no priest is necessary in order for this to be possible – although some people may find it psychologically helpful to confess out loud to someone else. In this view, the sole purpose of prayer for forgiveness is a psychological and meditative one. Confession is a matter of coming to human wholeness and of finding that one can cope with one's failures and not be handicapped by a legacy of guilt from the past.

Model 2

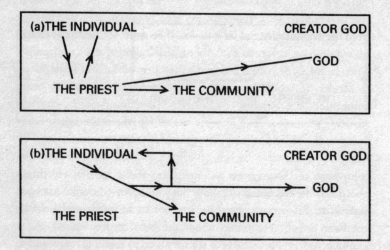

In Model 2(a), Anita will go to the priest to tell him about her sins. In Model 2(b) she will not feel that this is necessary.

In both these models God is involved, but it is the anti-realist God, not the creator God of traditional Christianity (if you are not clear about this, refer to the definitions at the beginning of this chapter). In Models 2(a) and 2(b) praying for forgiveness has the same psychological and therapeutic effects as set out in Model 1, but in addition Anita is reconciled to the community of which she is a part. In Model 2(a) this happens through the priest who, as the leader of the community, is able to grant reconciliation, whereas in Model 2(b) no priest is necessary, and the reconciliation between the individual and the community is direct.

The idea of someone being reconciled to the community to which he or she belongs may seem strange to some readers. An example may help to explain this. I once gave a talk to some Benedictine monks on the philosophic problems involved in prayer, and the following was one of the examples I used. Imagine that one of the monks had seduced a young girl. The *Sun* picked this up and it was splashed across the front page. The monk's action not only damaged himself but also inflicted very real damage on the community of which he was a member. He had, by his sin, alienated himself from the community and let it down. If he were to seek forgiveness, he would have to go to the Abbot, the leader of the community. Then he might be reconciled to the members of the brotherhood.

Model 2(b) could be similarly illustrated. Perhaps a sexual sin is committed by a member of a believing community. Their customs advocate public confession as the means by which the relationship between the individual and the community may be restored, and by which he or she may be accepted back into full membership and fellowship.

It must be recognised that the monk in my example who has sinned and who is reconciled back to the community may well feel comforted and forgiven, but questions do need to be asked about the girl who was seduced and who may have no community to support her. Sometimes there can be too great a concentration on the effects of sin on the sinner and not enough on the possibly graver effect of sin on the person who was sinned against. However, this is a wider issue that can be relevant to all models of praying for forgiveness.

Model 3

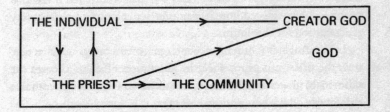

Andrew knows that he has sinned against the God who created him and to whom he owes total loyalty. He knows that he has been selfish. Instead of trying to come closer to God and to show others the love of God, he has been indifferent and hard, concentrating solely on his business and on increasing profits. He knows that he is like the people in the Bible whom Jesus criticised for putting money and material success before God. He knows that he has ignored God. He also knows that God still loves him, but he recognises the distance he has put between himself and God. He very much regrets his failings and therefore goes to the priest, confesses his sins and is absolved. He goes away content and at peace, knowing that because of the priest's absolution he can start again, and that his sins are forgiven by God.

The big difference between this model and Model 2 is that this one involves the creator God whilst Model 2 was relevant to the anti-realist's God. In this model, praying for forgiveness (i) has the same psychological effects as in Model 1, although the priest is necessary here to reassure the individual. In addition, (ii) the priest is the person who reconciles the individual to his or her community, which was a feature of Model 2(a). Also, (iii) the priest reconciles the individual to the creator God. It is important to notice, that in this view, reconciliation to the creator God takes place through the offices of the priest.

This view is a much more Catholic approach than the alternative below, which sees little role for the priest. The Catholic Church still insists on its members going to a priest for individual confession and absolution (indeed John Paul II has insisted that this is something that Catholics must do – general confessions in Church are not, in normal circumstances, sufficient). The Catholic will go to confession, the priest will give penance and will then absolve the individual of his or her sins, although genuine repentance is a necessary precondition for absolution.

In the Anglian Church, in which personal confessions are rare, only the priest can pronounce the absolution of sins, although the differences in wording between the occasions when the priest takes the service and when a lay reader takes it is a very small one. The priest will say:

> Almighty God, who forgives all who truly repent,
> have mercy upon you,
> pardon and deliver you from all your sins,
> confirm and strengthen you in all goodness,

and keep you in life eternal, through Jesus Christ our Lord. Amen. (*Alternative Service Book 1980*, p. 62).

A layperson taking the service will use precisely the same words, except that 'you' will be changed to 'us'. The alteration is significant. The use of 'you' means that on behalf of the creator God the priest is forgiving those attending the service. The use of 'we' means that all those attending the service are, together, coming before God to seek his forgiveness. The Anglican approach is to accept both models.

Model 4

Leah knows that God loves her and is her friend, but she also knows that the way she has acted has been appalling. She has ignored God, turned her back on her friend, acted in ways that deliberately shut him out of her life. She knows that God still loves her and she speaks to him in her prayer, saying how sorry she is for all the things she has done. She knows that her true happiness can only be found in re-establishing her relationship with God, which has been broken by her actions. She resolves anew only to act in such a way as God would approve of. She will show love, she will not be impatient, she will be less selfish. Having prayed, Leah feels and knows that God has forgiven her. She goes away refreshed and relaxed, secure in her relationship with God.

In this more typically Protestant view Leah, in praying for forgiveness, is seeking to re-establish her relationship with the creator God. She has sinned and has turned away from him, as if from a friend. The relationship of love – the two-way I/Thou relationship that should exist between the believer and the creator God – has been spoilt by her actions. Of course, God's love for Leah has not changed, but she has herself undermined the relationship. In praying for forgiveness, she is therefore recognising the breakdown in the relationship that has taken place and is seeking to re-establish the previous ties of love and friendship.

The closest parallel to this is my hurting a friend by some word or action. Because I have hurt him I have placed a barrier between myself and my friend. I can go to him and say: 'I'm sorry. I shouldn't have done that. I recognise that I have hurt you. Because I care for you I regret what I have done. Please, will you forgive me?' Then the relationship will be mended and the hurt will be a thing of the past. So it is with God. The believer goes to God, as if to a friend, to re-establish the lost relationship. He or she will be secure in the knowledge that forgiveness is available. After all, even good human friends can forgive, and God's love is much greater than that of any human. However, the believer will know that it is he or she who must move to re-establish the broken relationship. The person has turned away from God, and only he or she can choose to turn back again.

You will notice that the diagram above, unlike the diagram for Model 3, has an arrow coming back from God to the individual. This is necessary, because the creator God is held to respond to the individual who prays in much the same way as a friend would respond. Crucial to this model is the idea of a two-way personal relationship which is not a feature of Model 1 or Model 2 and which is less strongly emphasised in Model 3.

Vincent Brummer (*What Are We Doing When We Pray?*) helpfully discusses this fourth model of petitionary prayer. He draws a useful distinction between (i) an understanding of God's relation to the individual believer based on the idea of a two-way relationship or (ii) an understanding based on the idea of a contractual obligation or agreement. Brummer clearly favours the former model. He writes:

Whereas broken fellowship can only be restored by penitence

and forgiveness, broken agreements are restored by satisfaction, punishment or condonation. If we do not clearly distinguish agapeistic fellowship from an agreement of rights and duties, we will also tend to confuse penitence with punishment and forgiveness with condemnation ...

Penitential prayers in which we confess our sins to God and ask for his forgiveness, presuppose that the God to whom we pray is a personal Being with whom we may enter into a personal relationship ... If we were to interpret the relation between God and human persons in terms of rights and duties, this would either make prayers for divine forgiveness inappropriate, or turn them into acts which somehow merit the restoration of one's rights before God, or into requests for divine condonation or remission of penalty.

Brummer's point is significant. He is claiming that the believer's relationship with God can be looked at in two ways:

1 The believer's relationship with God can be regarded as being a contractual one, with punishment and penalties being imposed for infringement of the terms of the agreement. The believer is required to live up to certain standards set by God: he or she must develop the full potential of his or her human nature. Failure to do this will result in punishment, the most extreme forms of which are very nasty indeed. Brummer considers that this is a mistaken view, albeit one that is widely held.

2 Instead, Brummer considers that we should look at the relationship between God and believer as a two-way love-relationship. On this view, prayer for forgiveness involves seeking to re-establish a relationship that has been spoilt.

On this view, no priest is necessary. I do not have to go to a third party if I have hurt my friend – I go to him directly. Similarly, if the believer has sinned, he can go straight to God and seek his forgiveness. The psychological benefits to the individual seeking forgiveness are undoubted, but these effects come from feeling that the God-relationship has been restored. It is not simply a meditative technique.

This approach sees no real place for the community in praying for forgiveness, except insofar as all believers who belong to a community may recognise their own failures, fallibility and sinfulness and see themselves as fellow pilgrims on the road towards God. There is no particular need for each individual to be reconciled back into the community, because the community consists of individuals who are all sinners. They do not consider that failure or sin places the individual outside the community in such a way that he or she needs to be accepted back in once more.

All the four models we have considered are viable possibilities, although we have seen that they have different implications. It is hard to say that one is more plausible than another on philosophic grounds, once the different presuppositions are accepted. The key issue is this: which presuppositions are valid?

1 Does God exist as a wholly simple, timeless substance or everlasting Spirit – is God, in other words, the traditional creator God? If the answer is 'No', then Models 1, 2(a) or 2(b) apply; if it is 'Yes', then either Model 3 or Model 4 apply.

2 Does the believer have to be reconciled to his or her community in any formal way after committing sins? If the answer is 'No', then either Model 1 or 4 will apply; if it is 'Yes', then either Model 2 or 3 will apply.

3 Is a priest necessarily a part of the individual being forgiven? If the answer is 'No', then Models 1, 2(b) or 4 will apply; if it is 'Yes', then either Model 2(a) or 3 will apply.

The choices are ours to make, although we should recognise that these choices should involve some rational grounds. Therefore, before we choose which model of prayer for forgiveness to adopt we should give further careful consideration to the presuppositions.

Summary

We have analysed four possible ways in which believers understand praying for forgiveness. They are all rational and plausible, depending on which of the underlying preconceptions about (i) God, (ii) the believer's community, and (iii) the role of the priest are adopted. The different variables have been set out immediately above.

At the least, prayer is a meditative exercise with therapeutic effects. It may also involve reconciliation of the individual with the community to which he or she belongs. In addition, if God is held to exist as timeless substance or an everlasting Spirit, praying for forgiveness may involve reconciliation of the individual to the creator God.

Questions for consideration

a) Why is it important to pray for forgiveness?
b) Does it make any difference to what a believer is doing when he or she prays for forgiveness whether there is or is not a creator God?
c) Is it necessary for a priest to have any particular role in prayer for forgiveness? If so, why?
d) Can the religious community have any role in prayers for forgiveness? Is so, what role might this be?
e) 'In praying for forgiveness we seek to come to terms with our failings, and to orientate ourselves once more towards human wholeness.' Do you consider this a satisfactory definition? Give reasons.

SEVENTEEN
Miracles

Jesus is claimed to have turned water into wine; to have walked on water; to have fed five thousand people on five loaves and two fishes; to have raised Lazarus from the dead; to have cured a woman with a haemorrhage; to have restored people's sight; to have cured leprosy; to have made the lame walk; and, after being killed, to have risen from the dead on Easter Day. The Gospels are full of accounts of miracles. If one is going to take the Gospel writers at all seriously, then the miracle stories cannot be too quickly dismissed.

The Bible does not, however, provide a very clear starting point. Biblical scholars consider that some of the stories in the New Testament may have been added later; others may have been exaggerated accounts. And even if the accounts are true, this does not necessarily mean that miracles of this type occur today. Also, the Bible acknowledges that miracles can be performed not only by followers of the true God – the magicians who served Pharaoh could perform miracles just as impressive as those performed by Moses.

There are various possible definitions of a miracle and a number of alternatives will be considered in this chapter. Much will depend on the model of God with which one is working, for instance, if a miracle is defined in such a way that it represents an action by God, then this is only possible if one considers that there is a God who can act in the universe. In other words, it depends on a realist understanding of language about God. The first definition assumes that such a God exists:

1) A miracle is a transgression of the laws of nature brought about by God

David Hume defines a miracle as 'A transgression of a law of nature brought about by a particular volition of the Deity, or by the interposition of some invisible agent.' This is the classic understanding of a miracle and is sometimes referred to as the 'violation' concept of miracle since it involves a violation of the laws of nature. The miracles in the New Testament (see above) all seem to fit this category. God, or Jesus – to the Christian the two are, for the purposes of miracles, more or less interchangeable – acted and breached the normal understanding of natural law. Jesus' power to walk on water showed his mastery over the physical elements. God still intervenes today.

We do have a fairly accurate understanding of natural laws. To be sure, some of our ideas may be inaccurate, but on the whole we know the ways in which many of the natural laws operate. Richard Swinburne claims that we are justified in taking an event to be a violation of natural law if it is inconsistent with our whole understanding of the scheme of things. He says:

> We have to some extent good evidence about what are the laws of nature, and some of them are so well established and account for so much data that any modification of them which we could suggest to account for the odd counter-instance would be so clumsy and ad hoc as to upset the whole structure of science (*The Concept of Miracle*, Macmillan, 1970, p. 32).

Examples such as walking on water, the Resurrection and turning water into wine would seem to fit in well with Swinburne's understanding of a breach of natural law. To expect us to revise our understanding of natural law because of a single reported instance of someone walking on water seems unreasonable in the extreme.

There are real problems as to whether the classic understanding of a miracle should be accepted, and we are going to have to devote more attention to this definition of miracle than to any other. Two attacks on this definition need to be taken seriously.

David Hume

Hume asks us, as rational human beings, to balance on the one hand the improbability of miracles occurring and on the other hand the evidence that they have occurred. He claims that, if we do this, we will always come to the conclusion that it is more likely that natural laws have held good rather than that a miracle has occurred. Here is a paraphrase of Hume's argument:

> A wise man proportions his belief to the evidence. A miracle is the violation of the laws of nature and is therefore an event which past human experience is uniformly against. This in itself makes it overwhelmingly probable that the miracle did not occur, unless the testimony to its occurrence is of such superlative quality that it can seriously be weighed against our own uniform past experience.
>
> In fact, however, the testimony to miracles is not of this character at all. The standard of the witnesses to miracles is not high. The human capacity for accepting or believing that the unlikely has all too probably been at work, the stories of miracles derive from 'ignorant and barbarous places and nations' and, in any case, the miracle stories of different religions contradict each other. Consequently testimony to miracles can never establish them so that one could proceed from a proper assurance that they occurred to infer some theistic conclusions.

This is a famous statement and it is worth examining the claims Hume is making in some detail. He argues:

i. A miracle is a breach of a law of nature – an example would be a man walking on water, or water being changed into wine.

ii. Belief in miracles is not rational. For Hume, rationality involves the following principles:

- Proportioning our belief to the evidence available.
- Accepting that we have uniform past evidence for laws of nature. All our experience tells us that when people walk on water they sink; that the molecular structure of water cannot change into that of wine; that once someone has died, they do not rise from the dead

  It will always, Hume argues, be more rational to believe that the laws of nature continue to hold and that no miracles have occurred.

iii. Not only is belief in miracles (defined as breaches of the laws of nature) irrational, but the reports of witnesses are unreliable and untrustworthy. Hume says that a rational man would expect witnesses, if they were going to be considered to be reliable, to be educated and intelligent. They should have a reputation to lose and nothing to gain. In the case, for instance, of the New Testament miracle stories, the relatively ignorant fishermen had a great deal to gain from miracles, stories which would make their master appear in a good light. What is more:

- Human nature loves the fantastic. People love the idea of something unlikely happening. Many still claim to have experienced UFOs and others claim to see the Loch Ness monster. Some people lie, whilst many others are sincerely mistaken.
- Generally, reports of miracles come from ignorant and barbarous people. Primitive folklore has many tales of miracle and strange stories of the supernatural.

If, therefore, the poor testimony to miracles is put together with the unlikelihood that laws of nature have been breached, it will always be more sensible to reject reports of miracles than to believe them. This is, Hume considers, the obvious conclusion to be reached if we weigh the evidence on both sides.

iv. All religions claim miracles, so if one bases the truth of those religions on miracle stories then all religions have equal claims to truth. Assuming that different religions are not compatible, their differing miracle stories simply cancel out and provide, as Hume puts it, a 'complete triumph for the sceptic'.

All in all, therefore, Hume maintains that it should never be rational to believe in reports of miracles. Hume's argument has much to commend it, but if we examine his claims in closer detail, their effectiveness will be seen to be more limited than he may have imagined.

1 Hume talks of 'laws of nature' as if they were set in stone, thus implying that no natural law can ever be shown to be false. However, science advances by showing that our existing understandings of some natural laws are incorrect. Otherwise one would have to ignore any experiments that showed our present theories to be false. To be fair to Hume, he could restate his point here and maintain that one should only take account of evidence against a supposed natural law if this evidence could be duplicated under controlled laboratory conditions and predictive power. In other words, one should ignore what appear to be breaches of natural law, and should only take account of exceptions if an experiment which showed the natural law to be false could be repeated. The possibility must remain open, however, for laws of nature to be shown to be false, and this is something that Hume does not recognise.

2 Hume was working with Newton's understanding of natural laws being fixed. The modern understanding is, however, that what we consider to be natural laws are based on probabilities. At the fundamental particle level, chaos theory teaches us that the movement of particles is random and, therefore, exceptions to what are regarded as natural laws are possible. Hume's approach does not allow for this.

3 Hume only deals with reports of miracles. Nothing in his argument shows that one should ignore a miracle that one has experienced oneself. If Hume himself had experienced a miracle, he might well have believed it, even if he insisted on rejecting any second-hand reports.

4 Hume was writing at a time when the only support for miracle stories came from word-of-mouth reports. Today, claimed miracles are sometimes supported by scientific evidence. At Lourdes there have been 68 carefully attested claims that natural laws, as an independent team of doctors understand them, have been broken and the Church has therefore declared that a miracle has occurred. The evidence has been carefully sifted and documented by unbiased scientists working with the latest available medical equipment. Bones have regrown when all the evidence is that this cannot happen; terminal cancers have gone into permanent remission and many other inexplicable events have been clearly proved. Here, the doctors are exactly of the sort that Hume demanded: they have reputations to lose and the evidence in incontrovertible.

5 Neither Christianity, Islam nor Judaism has ever claimed that someone should believe solely on the basis of miracles. Jesus himself rejected any appeal to signs and wonders as evidence for his status. He rejected the Devil's temptation in the wilderness to perform a miracle by throwing himself down from the Temple, and also the temptation to save himself miraculously from the cross. When, therefore, a person considers whether belief in miracles is rational or not, he or she does not have to look on them as an unbiased observer. If someone believes in the existence of God on other grounds, it may therefore be rational to believe that God acts in the world to suspend natural law. What is *not* rational is to believe in any particular religion on the basis of reports of miracles alone. In this, at least, Hume's arguments appear convincing.

Anthony Flew also challenges the conventional idea of miracles and his work can be used to supplement that of Hume. Flew claims that although the evidence for extraordinary events at places like Lourdes is good, this does not prove that the extraordinary events have been brought about by the agency of God. Perhaps, instead, we may be dealing with evidence of the remarkable power of the human mind. A hundred years ago, video cameras, portable televisions and cellular radios would have been considered miraculous, yet they are part of today's routine technology. Similarly, psychology has helped us to understand much about the mind that has previously been wrapped in mystery. There is a great deal that we do not know about the human mind. It may well be possible that, under the right conditions, our minds can bring about changes in our bodies. Flew's claim is that breaches of what we understand to be natural law can occur but the proper response should be to spend more money on research rather than to say 'God did it.'

Moreover, another challenge now awaits those who consider that miracles represent acts by a divine agent against the laws of nature. This challenge is even more devastating and effective than that of Hume and it is put forward by a modern philosopher, Maurice Wiles.

Maurice Wiles

Wiles' position has already been referred to in the chapter on Prayer (p. 177) but his argument against miracles is strong. Wiles' proposal in *God's Action in the World* (SCM Press, 1986) is that 'the primary usage for the idea of divine action should be in relation to the world as a whole rather than to particular occurrences within it' (p. 28). He wants to speak of 'the world as a whole as a single act of God' (p. 29). He believes 'there are no good grounds for speaking of particular divine actions with respect to particular phenomena' (p. 34). He is claiming, in other words, that there is a single act of God – and this act encompasses the world as a whole. God never intervenes in the world by individual acts. Wiles continues:

If the direct action of God, independent of secondary causation, is an intelligible concept, then it would appear to have been sparingly and strangely used. Miracles must by definition be relatively infrequent or else the whole idea of laws of nature ... would be undermined, and ordered life as we know it would be an impossibility. Yet even so it would seem strange that no miraculous intervention prevented Auschwitz or Hiroshima, while the purposes apparently forwarded by some of the miracles acclaimed in traditional Christian faith seem trivial by comparison (p. 66).

In other words, Wiles challenges the idea of a God who would intervene in the ordered universe by bringing about a few bizarre miracles against the laws of nature. He is claiming that an interventionist God is a debased idea of God, effectively a God who would not be worthy of worship.

Wiles quotes Brian Hebblethwaite, who accepts the conceivability of miracle on philosophic grounds, but he is much more dubious about whether miracles, defined as breaches of laws of nature, ever occur:

> To suppose that God acts in the world by direct intervention just occasionally would be to raise all the problems which perplex the believer as he reflects on the problem of evil, about why God does not intervene more often. It would also prevent him from appealing to the God-given structures of creation, and their necessary role in setting creatures at a distance from their creator and providing a stable environment for their lives, as an explanation for the physical ills which can afflict God's creatures (B. Hebblethwaite, *Evil, Suffering and Religion*, Sheldon Press, 1976, pp.92–3).

Wiles sees, therefore, 'no need for the Christian believer to affirm any form of direct divine intervention in the natural order and good reasons for not doing so' (p. 69). A God that acted in some special cases and not in others would have an apparently arbitrary will, and this apparent arbitrariness would be a serious objection to the idea of miracles as direct intervention by God in the natural order. Because of this and because of Hebblethwaithe's points above, Wiles wants to 'deny to God the freedom to act without causal restraint in the world' (p. 80). This, he holds, does not depersonalise God at all, as the whole of creation is the act of God – which God does not act against by any form of intervention.

The idea of an interventionist God is, Wiles maintains, 'both implausible and full of difficulty for a reasoned Christian faith'. He is right about the difficulties – at least if we insist on a rational understanding. A God who intervenes at Lourdes to cure an old man from terminal cancer but does not act to save starving millions in Ethiopia; who helps the individual believer by giving him or her personal guidance about whether to take a new job or to sell his or her house, but does not prevent the mass murder of the Jews at Auschwitz, such a God needs, at the least, to face some hard moral questioning. Some may hold that this God is not worthy of worship.

Keith Ward in his book *Divine Action* replies to Wiles and claims that God can act in the world but does so only occasionally, as otherwise the whole order of creation would be disrupted. God would only act for the best but can, Ward maintains, be influenced by prayer to act in some cases and not in others. According to Ward, however, God's purpose in causing occasional miracles is not to reduce suffering but to build faith.

The challenges by Hume, Flew and Wiles against the whole idea of God acting to perform miracles are strong. If, however, one already believes in a God who created and sustains the universe and can interact with it, then belief in miracles becomes much more plausible. If one believes in such a God, and if one saw an event such as water being turned into wine or a dead man coming to life, then it might be entirely reasonable to assume that God had acted to bring the event about. The atheist or, indeed, agnostic may always consider it more reasonable to seek a rational, scientific explanation for any unexplained event, even if such an explanation is not currently available. If, however, God does, indeed, exist then there seems no reason why God cannot act – although the problem as to when God acts and why the actions are not more frequent remains.

2) A miracle is an event that is in accordance with the laws of nature but which the believer sees as being due to the action of God

This is what is sometimes referred to as a 'coincidence' miracle. Miracles under this heading do not transgress the laws of nature – they may be just part of the normal, natural order of the world, or they may be cases where God is seen to act through a human being (Aquinas' principle of 'double agency' would be relevant here The believer claiming a miracle under this heading is specifically claiming that the event in question is being brought about by the action of God. It is not just a 'disclosure event' which is being seen in a certain way by the believer. God, on this view, is an agent who acts in the world.

The best-known example of such a providential miracle may be that described by R. F. Holland (*American Philosophical Quarterly*, 1965, p. 43). Imagine a child whose toy car has become stuck on a level crossing. The mother sees the child and also sees that an express train is hurtling towards the crossing. Suddenly, the train's emergency brakes are applied and it shudders to a halt only a short distance from the child. The mother utters a prayer of thanks to God for this miracle. However, subsequent investigation shows that the driver fainted. The faint was explainable on routine medical grounds, without any recourse to divine intervention. The mother, however, in spite of the medical explanation that is given to her, never ceases to believe that God acted to stop the train in order to save her child. This miracle – if miracle it indeed was – is not against the laws of nature. Instead, God is held to have acted through the laws of nature.

Another example may be helpful:

Life magazine reported (March 27, 1950, p. 19) that all fifteen members of a church choir in Beatrice, Nebraska, came at least ten minutes too late for their weekly choir practice which was supposed to start at 7.20p.m. on March 1, 1950. They were astonishingly fortunate because at 7.25p.m. the building was destroyed by an explosion. The reasons for the delay of each member were fairly commonplace; none of them was marked by the slightest sign of a supernatural cause. However, nothing remotely resembling the situation that all members were prevented from being on time on the same occasion had ever happened before. Furthermore, this singular event took place precisely when it was needed, on the very night when they would otherwise have perished. Consequently some people were inclined to see the incident as a clear case of divine intervention and a compelling manifestation of God's care and power for everyone to see. How else could one explain such a spectacular coincidence which turned out to be the deliverance of people who were regarded as the most pious, and most intensely devoted to any church-associated work, and thus the most truly worthy to be saved, in a manner which (though it did not violate any law of nature) was too startling to be mere happenstance?[1] (George Schlesinger, 'Miracles', in P. Quinn and C. Taliaferno's *A Companion to Philosophy of Religion*, Blackwell, 1997, p. 362.)

This can illustrate the difference between the realist and the anti-realist understanding. The realist claims that the word 'miracle' is correctly applied if and only if (this is written 'iff') the event is brought about by the action of God – in the case of Holland's example above, if and only if the driver's faint, or in the second example, if the people being late for choir practice, was caused by God. The anti-realist, by contrast, holds that the word 'miracle' is correctly applied if it coheres with the understanding of miracle within the religious form of life of the mother and the community to which she belongs. The anti-realist would claim that it would be true to describe the event as a miracle if this made sense within the mother's form of life. The dividing line is a fine one. It can be spelt out more clearly by means of these two statements:

1 'This event is a miracle because, although it is in accordance with natural law, it has particular religious significance.'

2 'This event is a miracle because it is brought about by a specific action on the part of the timeless or everlasting God.'

The realists (i.e. those who advocate the view of miracle given under the present heading), are committed to *both* statements 1 *and* 2. The anti-realists (i.e. those who advocate the view of miracle give under the next heading) are only committed to statement 1.

On both understandings of miracle, any event may be described as a miracle and much is going to depend on 'the eye of the beholder'. There is no point in looking for further evidence to help us decide between the realist and anti-realist interpretations. There is no disagreement about the facts. The disagreement is about their interpretion and what it means to claim that it is true that a miracle has occurred.

3) A miracle is an inexplicable event which, within the form of life of the believing community, is termed a miracle

The first point to note here is that there is no assumption that God acted to bring the event about. On this view, whether or not something is a miracle depends entirely on how event(s) are seen by different people. This is an anti-realist view – the term 'miracle' is correctly applied if the word makes sense within the form of life of the religious believer. The term does not have to correspond to any particular state of affairs in order to be correctly applied (it is this factor that distinguishes this approach from that taken under the previous heading).

The Dominican priest Gareth Moore, in his book *Believing in God, a Philosophical Essay*, has produced an interesting view of miracles which could be included under this heading. Moore is firmly committed to the view that God is nothing. This, as we have previously seen, is not a restatement of Aquinas' view that God is no thing, but rather a commitment to the view that the word 'God' does not refer to any being at all. God is not an agent who created and sustains the universe. For Moore, a miracle occurs where there is no explanation – it is specifically not an act of a creator God. He says of a typical cure obtained at Lourdes:

> Much of the investigation is concerned with ruling out possible causes for the cure, showing what has not caused it; and it is certainly not proved to be a miracle by the discovery of the cause for the cure and its subsequent identification as God (p. 226).

> to say that God brought it about is not to say that somebody brought it about ... God causes what nothing causes (p. 223).

If, therefore, we have a situation where there is no explanation at all, the believer will rightly call this a miracle, whilst the non-believer will say that the phenomenon merely has no explanation. The non-believer, 'who has no context available to him to fit the event into, therefore simply finds it baffling' (p. 225). The believer 'does believe that God is responsible for it but to believe that is not to believe that *somebody* is responsible for it (p. 225). The believer has a context, a form of life and a language with which to explain events that the non-believer describes as inexplicable. Whereas the non-believer uses terms such as 'baffling', the believer uses terms such as 'God' and 'miracle'.

For Moore, God is not an agent, and so in his view it is wrong to think of miracles as events brought about by a creator God who acts in the world. Moore's account is interesting and it makes sense, given the anti-realist position (it is important to remember Moore's maxim, given in the final sentence of his book: 'people do not discover religious truths, they make them'). However, his account depends on God *not* being timeless substance or an everlasting Spirit, since both these are agents who can and do bring about effects in the universe which they are held to have created and still sustain. If 'God exists' is true within the form of life of the believing community, or if language about God tells us something about a different way in which we can live life, then Moore's account may be plausible, although it does confine miracle to the realm of bizarre happenings.

Moore points out that miracles generally only occur following a series of disasters. If God really was an agent of some sort, Moore asks, why does God allow situations to arise which make it necessary for miracles to be performed, so that things can be put right? To think of miracles as actions by God is in effect to say that this agent God has made a mess of the series of events that has led up to the present need for a miracle.

Moore gives a graphic example that illustrates his position well. A young boy is lying under a cliff face and a boulder falls towards him. Suddenly, three feet from hitting the boy, the boulder stops and hovers in midair The boy is pulled clear and scientists are called out to carry out tests on the boulder. There are no wires, no strings, no force fields that can be detected. The mother, who is a religious believer, gives thanks to God. For Moore, this event was not caused by God – instead, it is an inexplicable event and, in the form of life of the believing community, 'miracle' is the word given to an inexplicable event.

For Moore a miracle is not an action by an agent God – it is an event that has no explanation at all. That is what the word 'miracle' means. This is an attractive view, but many believers would want to reject Moore's thesis and to claim that miracles *are* actions by an agent God who brings about effects in the world. Those who hold this view would opt for the previous definitions of miracle, although they would then have to face the intellectual difficulties to which these give rise.

4) A miracle as a change for the better in a person

In Dostoevsky's *The Brothers Karamazov* we read of Alyosha, a young and holy monk who is studying under the elder monk, Zossima Alyosha, and has joined Zossima's monastery because of his influence. In the town near the monastery is a lady of somewhat dubious virtue called Grushenka who has had her eyes on Alyosha but has made no progress with him at all. Then Zossima dies, and the monastic community and the people from the village gather round his bed. The expectation in Russia at this time is that if a very holy person dies, his body will not decompose. For three days those around the bed of the dead Zossima wait patiently. Eventually it becomes obvious that there is a smell – Zossima's body is decomposing. Aloysha is devastated. The man whom he looked up to and revered was obviously not as holy as he thought. Alyosha leaves the monastery and finds his way to Grushenka's house. He is totally vulnerable, and one expects Grushenka to comfort him in her own way. Instead, Grushenka puts Alyosha together spiritually – the transformation in her is quite remarkable. It is transformations such as this, in possibly the most unlikely people and situations, that Sutherland (in *God, Jesus and Belief*, Blackwell, 1983) regards as truly being miracles.

Sutherland wants to claim that human beings are free and always have the capacity for great good. The ability of the good to break through in any situation is where the true power of miracle lies. This view of miracle does not demand a creator God and is a view that can be held by supporters of any of the three views of God that we have been examining. Supporters of God as an everlasting Spirit or as timeless substance may ascribe the transformation in a human being to the power of God – although if they do this, they will have to be careful to ensure that their interpretation of God's action does not undermine human freedom.

Summary

We have looked at four possible definitions of miracle:

1 A miracle as a transgression of the laws of nature brought about by God

2 A miracle as an event which is in accordance with the laws of

nature but which the believer sees as being due to the action of God.

3   A miracle as an inexplicable event which, within the form of life of the believing community, is termed a miracle.

4   A miracle as a change for the better that can take place in a human person in the most unlikely situation.

Which definition you choose will depend on how you define God. The first alternative clearly requires a God who can act in the universe. The second definition may or may not require such a God. The third specifically rules out a miracle as being an action of God. The definition of miracle as a breach of natural law suffers particular problems when it forms part of a rational Christian faith. If miracles are arbitrary or inexplicable acts against the laws of nature by an agent God, then there are real moral questions to be asked about whether this is a God worthy of worship. Some believers may maintain, however, that they still want to affirm the existence of the creator God and the ability of this God to act in the world, even if they cannot understand the basis on which this God chooses to act.

Questions for consideration

a) What do you consider to be the most convincing definition of a miracle?
b) What are the difficulties in maintaining that God acts in the world to bring about effects that would not otherwise have happened?
c) Does something being a miracle depend entirely on the way it is seen by believers?
d) Is it ever rational to accept reports of a miracle that breaches known natural laws?
e) If someone you love becomes seriously ill from an incurable disease, would you hope or pray for a miracle? Give your reasons and explain what you would hope for.

EIGHTEEN

Eternal Life

He has made everything beautiful in its time:
Also he has put eternity into man's mind,
Yet so that he cannot find out what God has done
from the beginning to the end (Ecclesiastes 3:11).

The view one takes of God will largely determine the view one takes of what it means to talk about eternal life. There are two main possibilities:

1 Eternal life as a different quality of life here and now, in this world.
2 Eternal life as a different quality of life here and now, in this world, as well as a personal survival of death.

Eternal life as a different quality of life

Religious believers have too often stressed the idea of eternal life as something that occurs at death. However, the Christian tradition has always maintained that there is more to it than this. Eternal life involves a change in the way the individual lives. Believers talk of a 'new birth' into a new way of looking at and approaching life. Suddenly the priorities shared by so many people in the world no longer seem important, and life takes on a different quality. It is no longer power, money or material possessions that matter, but rather compassion, love, relationships with people and the higher values. As the Danish philosopher and theologian Søren Kierkegaard put it:

'Immortality cannot be a final alteration that crept in, so to speak, at the moment of death as the final stage. On the contrary, it is a changelessness that is not altered by the passage of the years ... If there is something eternal in a man it must be able to exist and be grasped within every change' (*Purity of Heart*, Harper and Row, 1948, pp. 35–6).

Kierkegaard is not denying life after death, but he is calling attention to the Christian claim that human beings can 'live in the eternal' in this world. Christian anti-realists talk of eternal life solely as a different quality of life here and now. They dismiss belief in a life after death. By living the holy life, human beings are enabled to overcome trivialisation, and to be grounded in the eternal. In other words, to live life for others and to be committed to self-sacrificial love rather than to selfishness and materialism enables us to 'live in the eternal' by grounding our life in values that endure when all around us changes. D. Z. Phillips maintains the eternal quality of an individual's life is its timeless quality of moral excellence. Talk of the immortality of the soul refers to a person's relation to the self-effacement and love of others involved in dying to the self – it does not refer to post-mortem existence.

The person whose inner life is orientated correctly, who is with passion and commitment seeking to live the good life, seeking to be kind, compassionate and gentle and to live for others is, no matter what happens, invulnerable. He or she is 'living in the eternal' and cannot be harmed, as nothing can take away this inner orientation. However things go in the world, the person whose life is grounded in the eternal cannot be overcome.

It is important to recognise that the idea of eternal life as a different quality of life now is common to all Christians, whatever their view of God. Many, however, want to say more that this.

Eternal life as the timeless Beatific Vision

We have previously seen that Roman Catholic theology affirms God is outside time and outside space. This has important implications for the way that Catholic theologians look at life after death. St Thomas Aquinas used Aristotle's idea of the separation of soul and body to explain the nature of human beings. For Aquinas, the *soul* is an individual *spiritual substance* (in other words, it can exist by itself), but it is also the form of the whole body. In Aristotelian philosophy, the form of a thing is that which remains unchanged in spite of the outward changes. Thus the form of 'treeness' would remain unchanged in spite of the changes in an individual tree. Aquinas considered that both body and soul together were needed to make a full human person, although the soul can survive death by itself.

Many people misunderstand Aquinas here. Aquinas and the Catholic Church, which has largely followed him, do *not* say that a person is made up of a soul and a body, and that after death the soul, which is the real person, survives. This is a straightforward *dualist* view. (A dualist holds that a human person is made up of two separate components, soul and body, which are independent of each other and yet interact in this world.) The dualist approach means that our identity lies in our soul, whilst our bodies are almost irrelevant. Plato was a dualist, and this led him to have a fairly low opinion of human bodies and the physical world as a whole, as the ultimate destiny for man was for the 'real me' to survive death as a disembodied soul. This is not the view of Aquinas nor that of the Catholic Church.

In Aquinas' view, soul and body are both needed to make a full human individual. The soul is in the body, just as God is present throughout the world. Aquinas says: 'all man's soul is in all his body and again all of it is in any part of his body, in the same way as God is in the world' (*Summa Theologiae* 1a, 93 3). The soul is present in every part of the body; it is not a 'separate something', hidden away somewhere, which somehow interacts with the body.

Aquinas held that, when we die, our souls survive and go to hell, to purgatory or to the Beatific Vision (there is another destination, limbo, which I will not deal with here). It is important to be clear on the difference between these:

1 Hell is temporal, in other words, time passes in hell. Aquinas maintained that those destined for hell suffer exclusion from God's presence and also eternal torment, pain and punishment. This punishment continues for ever and ever, as the human body could not stand the pain required if the period were to be shorter and the pain more intense. Modern writers tend to play down the punishment side of hell and instead see it as the place to which those people go who have deliberately, out of self-will, turned away from God.

2 Many souls pass to purgatory. Purgatory is the place, Catholic theology maintains, where individuals undergo purification and punishment pending their entry into their final end. It is, effectively, a 'holding state' where the soul is purged of the sins committed on earth. Only the wholly perfected and worthy souls are fit for the Beatific Vision. Purgatory is temporal – time passes there. Aquinas held that, after death, the guilt of venial sin is done away with by God by an act of pure charity. But the individual still has to undergo the punishment for his or her sins. The smallest pain in purgatory is greater than the greatest pain that can be experienced on earth, but it is relieved because everyone who goes there knows that they will eventually pass to the Beatific Vision of God, which is held to be the highest joy. Today less emphasis tends to be placed on the punishment that takes place in purgatory and more on the growth and development that may take place. Also, Catholic theology has moved away from speaking too literally about the number of days of relief from pain and suffering in purgatory that can be gained for oneself or others through good works. In fact, since the Second Vatican Council in 1965 few Catholic theologians have talked of purgatory at all. However, in 1998 Pope John Paul II confirmed that it was a central part of Catholic teaching and also said that time in purgatory could be lessened by, for instance, going on pilgrimage.

There is, however, a problem with this. The soul goes to purgatory, but Aquinas specifically says, *Anima mea non est ego* (my soul is not I). As we have seen above, a human person is the unity of body and soul. Aquinas considers that all those in purgatory receive a new and glorified body at some time when their sins have been sufficiently cleansed. The problem is that if I am in purgatory and it is my soul that is in purgatory, then I must be my soul. However, Aquinas says that I am not my soul, or at least, my soul is not fully me. Now either Peter Vardy is in purgatory or he is not. If he is, then Peter Vardy is his soul. And yet Aquinas denies this.

What is more, surely the pains and punishment that the individual has to undergo in purgatory require a body so that they can be experienced. Individual souls, however, have no bodies in purgatory.

Aquinas says that the soul is not 'fully me', and the real issue is whether we can make sense of this. Can the 'I' which I am now, be only partly this 'I' in purgatory until it receives a new and glorified body? Can I be only partly me? This seems a difficult position to justify.

When the punishment/perfection in purgatory has been completed, the souls that are there receive a new and glorified body and this is in preparation for

3 The timeless Beatific Vision. According to Catholic teaching, this is the final end for humankind. This Beatific Vision may vary between individuals, but it is completely satisfying. Those who attain this vision will share God's knowledge (except for God's motives and intentions, to which no one shall have access). As the Beatific Vision is timeless, it will never, never, ever change – it is the unchanging vision of God. There is, therefore, no idea here of a heavenly society in which Aunt Mable may meet Uncle Fred.

This idea of the timeless Beatific Vision may well have been influenced by Plato's belief that the final end for human beings was the contemplation of unchangeable Beauty, which was one of the Forms (see p. 18). The problem with this view is that Aquinas holds that the soul receives a new and glorified body at the Second Coming. However, if I, Peter Vardy, have a body, and if I need a body in order to be Peter Vardy, then I cannot become timeless. If I have a body, time must necessarily pass, and if time passes I cannot be timeless. There does, therefore, seem to be a real difficulty here. *Either* I have a body, in which case I cannot be timeless, *or* I become timeless, in which case I cannot have a body. Real questions arise as to whether it is Peter Vardy who is enjoying the timeless Beatific Vision.

When Jesus rose from the dead, he most certainly had a body, even though it was a special body that could pass through walls. He talked with the disciples, he ate food and was very much a temporal figure. If Jesus had retained this body, he could not have become timeless. After the Ascension, therefore, Jesus must have lost his post-Resurrection body in order to become the timeless Second Person of the Trinity. There is one reply that the Catholic theologian could make, that is, to claim that the new and glorified body is not to be understood univocally, but is rather a body in an analogous sense. It is true that human beings who reach the timeless Beatific Vision will have a body, but we do not know what it means for them to have a body. This, obviously, means that there is very little content indeed to the claim that we are embodied, but it does at least prevent the position from being an obvious contradiction.

This approach has two major attractions. First of all, an individual's soul (which is the form of his or her whole body) survives death and therefore establishes the link between this life and the next one. Peter Vardy survives death because it is Peter Vardy's soul that survives. Secondly, this view has a final end for human beings in the timeless, Beatific Vision of God. As we have seen, however, the problems are also considerable.

Eternal Life as life after death in a heavenly society

In the previous section we considered one way of looking at a human being which might give content to talk of our surviving death, that is, if the soul is the form of the whole body. There are, however, two alternatives which are often adopted by Protestant theologians who usually, although not always, work with an everlasting rather than a wholly simple and timeless view of God.

Both alternatives involve a heavenly society of some sort, but they differ because there are two possible understandings of what it means to be a human person.

Soul/body dualism

Straightforward soul/body dualism, which we defined in the previous section, is the model of personhood favoured by both Plato and Descartes. The soul is the real me and it is trapped in the body, which it drives like a ghost in a machine (as Gilbert Ryle puts it in his book *The Concept of Mind*, Penguin, 1970, which rejects this view). Those who maintain that soul and possibly mind (the two are not necessarily the same) are distinct from the body have different ideas about their interrelationship. Possibilities include the following:

1 The idea that souls are pre-existent and survive death, passing, perhaps, to a different realm before being united to a new body. Wordsworth captured something of the flavour of a pre-existent soul in his poem 'Intimations of immortality from recollection of early childhood':

> *Our birth is but a sleep and a forgetting:*
> *The soul that rises with us, our life's star,*
> *hath had elsewhere its setting*
> *and cometh from afar:*
> *Not in entire forgetfulness*
> *and not in utter nakedness*
> *but trailing clouds of glory do we come,*
> *from God who is our home …*

Wordsworth is here claiming that our soul, which comes into our body at conception or at some other early stage, has previously inhabited other bodies. We remember something of our previous lives (hence 'not in entire forgetfulness …') but, the poem continues, we lose these memories as we grow up.

2 *Creationism*, which is the belief that each soul is created by God

and attached to the growing foetus at a certain point. This is one reason why some believers are so concerned about embryo research. These are, however, problems as to when God implants this soul. Up to 14 days after the sperm and the egg unite to form a single unit (when the hairline appears), this unit may divide and may then come together again. If, therefore, the soul is implanted by God at the moment of conception, then what happens when the unit divides? Do we then have two souls? If so, what happens if and when the two parts come together again? (These issues are dealt with in more detail in *The Puzzle of Ethics*.)

3 *Traducianism*, which is the belief that a soul is created naturally when a man and woman make love as part of normal conception. This latter theory was developed by some of the Latin Church Fathers, such as Tertullian, who saw the soul as the substance which God breathed into Adam and which was passed down through the many generations of human beings by continuous division. It eventually came to be held to be a heresy.

There are severe problems with dualism, including the following:

1 How do souls and bodies interact? Descartes maintained that the interaction was through a little gland at the back of the head called the pineal gland, but this has been discredited. The disembodied soul is meant to be 'driving' the machine, which is the body, but it is far from clear what the mechanism is that enables this to happen. Also, this whole approach tends to denigrate the value of the physical in human beings, emphasing the soul as that which is most important. It tends to point us away, therefore, from a holistic view of what it is to be a human being.

2 What is the relation between soul and the mind/brain? We know that brain states can be affected by our bodies and that drugs can easily affect our minds. An operation can alter a person's whole personality and memory. Given that the brain is the seat of our emotions, memory and actions, does this mean that our souls are

similarly affected? Could my soul possibly survive if my brain does not?

3 In *The Concept of Mind* Gilbert Ryle rejected all talk about souls, since it was based on what he termed a 'Category Mistake'. He gave two examples, of which the second is the more interesting. First, imagine showing a foreigner around a university. You show him the college buildings, the chapels, the libraries, the staff and the students. He sees all this but then says: 'Yes, I have seen all these things, but where is the university?' The mistake he is making is to think that the university is something on top of all those things he has seen.

The second example is that of a foreigner looking at a game of cricket. He sees the bowlers, the batsmen, the wicketkeeper, the fielders and the umpires but then says: 'I have seen all these people, but where is the team spirit?' Again, the mistake he makes is to think that 'team spirit' is something on top of all those things he has seen. So, Ryle argues, it is with talk of the soul. The soul is not an extra something on top of the intentional actions of a human person. To talk of a soul is to talk about the way a person acts and responds to other people; it is not to talk of a disembodied ghost of some sort.

4 Could one have a society of disembodied souls? H. H. Price, in an article entitled 'Survival and the Idea of Another World' (in Donnelly's *Language, Metaphysics and Death*, Fordham University Press, 1978), invites us to imagine what such a society would be like. He thinks it would have to be an 'image world' or a dream world into which we would carry our memories. We would be trapped within our memories and would thus in some ways create our own heaven or hell. We would be able to communicate telepathically with like-minded disembodied souls, but that would be all. As we would have no bodies we could not speak, hear, feel or experience in any other way. The laws operating in this post-mortem image world would be those of psychology rather than physics.

The picture Price paints is conceivable, but not particularly attractive, and it would be likely to be a boring existence with little eventual point to it. There would be little that would be creative or life-giving in such a world. The individual disembodied mind would not be capable of acting in relation to its environment.

5   How could my soul be me? Peter Vardy is a living human person who has a body, brain, sensory organs, emotions and feelings. It is not at all clear in what way a disembodied soul with none of these physical attributes could still be me.

There may, however, be an alternative conception of a soul which traditional arguments do not adequately represent. In the film *Lost in Space* a family is marooned in space in their spaceship which has become lost. They come across another spaceship that appears derelict and most of the family set out to explore it. The family includes a young boy who is a genius with electronics and he has programmed a robot to accompany the family whilst he stays on their ship. He can view what is happening through the robot's eyes. The family, attacked by alien spiders, fight a rearguard action as they make their way to the airlock. The young boy gets into a virtual-reality suit and, through this, controls the robot from the family's ship. The robot (or, rather, the boy 'in' the robot) holds off the spiders whilst the family escape. Finally the robot is overwhelmed by the spiders and is dragged down to be destroyed; the boy 'steps out' of the robot by stepping out of the virtual reality suit. The boy was totally 'in' the robot while it was operational. He was aware of what it was aware of and could control it as if it was his own body. When he 'stepped out' he was fully himself although the robot had 'died'.

Something like this is represented by the ancient Egyptian idea of a 'ka' or spiritual body that can separate from the early body. It is at least possible that this might provide a model for a new understanding of dualism which is rather different from the classical understanding of Plato and Descartes. The soul would not be a 'separate something' but the whole individual who is fully 'in' all parts of the person when alive but can 'step out' of the body when the person dies.

Nevertheless, the problems with dualism are considerable and it is by no means the most popular of the theories currently on offer to explain what it is to be a person and what it might mean for a person to survive death. Specifically, it is an understanding of personhood that has been rejected by Christian theology since Jesus is held to have risen from the dead embodied and, also, all the Christian creeds speak of the resurrection of the body as being central to life after death. It is surprising, however, how prevalent dualism is amongst people who have not thought through its problems.

The person as a person

This second version of the idea of a heavenly society after death is a *monistic* view. Whereas dualism affirms that there are two separate substances, soul and body, monism claims that there is only one. It holds that a person is a person and that one cannot analyse a person into bits. We do not have a separate soul; rather, to talk of a soul is to talk of the way we act and react to other people (Gilbert Ryle, referred to above, is a monist). If we take a holistic view of what it is to be a person, it means that, if we are to survive death as individuals, we must survive with our present identity retained. We must survive death as persons.

Advocates of this view can still talk of a person's soul, but by this they do not mean a 'separate something' mysteriously added onto his or her physical body and in some obscure way interacting with it. Talk of a person's soul is seen as a way of valuing the self. A person's individuality – to which talk of his or her soul refers – is formed by interaction and relationships with others. We can, of course, turn away from the possibility of developing the spiritual side of our nature: we can become cold and hard. Someone might say, referring to a colleague at work: 'She has no soul – she never cares for others. She just treats them as objects and never as individuals.' On this view, talk of souls is talk about personality. A person's soul could still be seen as God-given insofar as his or her whole personality and individuality depend on God.

This monistic view immediately creates problems. If Annabel

dies, the person that is Annabel lies dead on the floor. There is no separate soul that floats off somewhere else. Annabel was a person and Annabel is now dead. On the face of it, therefore, this approach seems bleak to those who advocate the idea of personal resurrection. However, the position is not as simple as this. Jesus, after all, was a person, and he died. His dead body was taken down from the cross and sealed in the tomb. Jesus was as dead as dead could be, and the disciples' faith in him was at an end. Yet Jesus rose from the dead, so it has traditionally been claimed, on Easter Day.

Christianity has, since the early centuries when the beliefs of the Church were first formulated, always affirmed the resurrection of the body. This was really a remarkable thing for the Church to affirm. The world in which the early Christians lived was largely dominated by Greek philosophic thought and this tended, although not universally, to think in terms of the soul surviving death. It would have been so easy and so apparently logical for Christianity to take the same line. Actually to claim that the body survived death in the face of the very clear evidence that dead bodies rotted and decayed could easily have made Christianity appear absurd.

There were various reasons for this Christian position. One of them was the belief that Jesus appeared to his disciples after his death, not as a disembodied spirit but as a resurrected person who could walk and talk with his friends and could even eat food with them. He was, however, a special kind of person, since he could appear in a locked room. Pre-mortem Jesus seemed remarkably similar to post-mortem Jesus, even down to the imprint of the nails in his hands.

Also, Christianity has never denied the importance of the physical world, which was a tendency of some dualist followers of Plato. The incarnation is about God taking human flesh and making this flesh, and with it the world we live in, holy. The physical is not in some way a second-class category in comparison with spiritual, disembodied souls, although it must be admitted that some Christian writers have thought in these terms.

The claim that a person survives death as an individual obviously raises the crucial issue of identity. How do we know that the

Principal of Heythrop College who dies is the same as the person who rises to life again? Bernard Williams (in *Language, Metaphysics and Death*, Donnelly, ed.) argues that the one sure test of personal identity is spatio-temporal continuity. The one thing that a baby, a young girl, a mature woman and an old lady have in common is that their bodies have followed the same space/time track. The baby gradually developed over time to become the old lady. Bernard Williams' approach would clearly rule out survival of death, as the space/time track is broken by death.

John Hick (in *Death and Eternal Life*, Collins, 1976) gives several examples which he maintains count against Williams' claims. He asks us to imagine someone lecturing in London, and then suddenly disappearing, only to reappear in New York. The person's spatio-temporal timetrack would be broken. Most people would, however, be willing to say it was the same person if appearance, memory and other details were in all apparent respects the same. Again, if a person dies on this earth but a duplicate of him or her comes to life on the planet Juno, we should also be prepared to recognise this as being the same person. We do not need, therefore, spatio-temporal continuity in order to guarantee survival of death.

Hick considers that a person is an indissoluble continuity. He rejects the idea of the soul as separate from the body, and with it the idea of the soul surviving death. Instead, he is advancing a replica theory. The duplicate person that comes to life in heaven is an exact replica of the person who died here on earth. God is, therefore, held to create in another space an exact psycho-physical replica of the deceased Principal of Heythrop. This is an attractive solution, as it enables us to avoid the complexities of the relation between the soul and the body. The person who survived death would be recognisably similar to the one who died and would have the same memories as the deceased individual.

Hick does not, however, take seriously enough the distinction between (i) the same person, and (ii) an identical person. The former implies a one-to-one relation between the person who has died and the person who survives. The latter, on the other hand, leaves open the possibility of a one-to-many relation. In other words, if we accept that all that is required is for a duplicate of us to be created when we die, why could not many identical copies be created? If the Principal of Heythrop College died and a hundred duplicates were created, all looking identical and all with the same memories, I would not be able to say that any one of them was the same person as the person who had died.

Williams makes the point that memory could not count as the sole necessary criterion for identity, as we could imagine several identical bodies all being given identical memories. If someone came in claiming to be Guy Fawkes, and this person had all Guy Fawkes' memories, we would not be willing to grant that he was Guy Fawkes. If we were willing to grant this, then many people could each have the same memories, and they could not *all* be Guy Fawkes!

If we are to preserve the idea of personal survival, there must be some criterion for establishing a one-to-one relationship between the Principal of Heythrop who dies and whoever it is who rises from the dead. If we do not have a soul – which, of course, would neatly fulfill the task of maintaining this continuity – then there appears to be no such continuity.

In my book *God of our Fathers* (published by Darton, Longman and Todd in 1987, but now out of print), I put forward the suggestion of a parallel between the idea of resurrection and the way my personal computer functions. In my college office I type out comments on my students' essays on this computer. These comments are stored on the computer's hard drive. If one of my students were to lose the essay comments I could, by pressing a button, print out an identical copy. Everything on the copy would be exactly the same – spelling, phrasing, punctuation and layout. The only difference would be that the second set of essay comments would be printed on a different piece of paper to the first. If I wished, I could transmit the comments by a radio signal to a satellite. From there the signal would be bounced back to Sydney, where an identical set of comments could be printed out.

A similar process might, I argued, happen to us after death. The creator God knows each of us intimately. God knows our detailed specification, including all our DNA and our memories. So when someone dies God could, using new materials, reproduce that person. St Paul talks of us having a new and glorified body, and there could be parallels here, possibly with defects in our bodies being rectified. Critics will, of course, say that I have not solved the one-to-one problem. God has created an identical copy, but if God has created one copy God could create many. My critics could claim that the parallel with the computer shows my error, as I could print out as many copies of the essay comments as I wished, and they would not be the original comments.

I did, in fact, deal with this point in my original argument. What my critics fail to take into account is that we are dealing here with God. God would simply not allow more than one person to be created for every person that died. If God did so, then identity would be destroyed, and this does not happen. This still seems to me to be persuasive, although it is not foolproof. It is true that, on this earth spatio-temporal continuity may be the one sure test of identity, but this is no reason why the same test has to be applied across the boundary line of death.

On this basis, the believer could claim that the individual would survive death as an individual. The new individual would be embodied, since having a body is an integral part of my being who I am. Bodies are, however, temporal and spatial, so this view would imply that life after death is also temporal and spatial. Heaven would, on this basis, be an everlasting kingdom under the lordship of Christ. God, seen as an everlasting Spirit, would be constantly present there. This would be a society filled with love and with all the negative and evil elements found in this world removed.

The world we live in now could be a place where we decide what sort of people we are going to become. We can choose to make ourselves selfish, greedy and interested solely in our own pleasures. In so doing we would be turning away from God and also from love and thus place ourselves, both in this world and after death, in permanent exile from God. The contrast would be with those who seek to develop their ability to love, who seek to develop the higher virtues and who, through their actions, become people who can love and care for others. Our ultimate destiny, on this basis, lies in fellowship with God in a heavenly kingdom – but we, being free, have the right to decide whether this is the destiny we wish to choose. This is not, of course, a fashionable view, but it is a view that some Christians at least still hold, and it does not seem philosophically incoherent.

Summary

Christianity has always maintained that, at the minimum, eternal life involves a different quality of life here and now. To 'live in the eternal' is to be born again into a new way of living and approaching life. Whatever view of God you adopt, this can be affirmed.

If, in addition to a different quality of life in this world, eternal life is held to involve personal survival of death, then this can take three forms:

1 Where the soul is the form of the whole body and becomes temporarily separated from the body on death, but is reunited with a new and glorious body at some time after death when the individual's sins have been purged.

2 Straightforward mind/body dualism in which the real 'I' is the soul, which survives death to enter into a form of disembodied existence.

3 The view that a person dies, and later has to be resurrected. On this view there are identity problems. In particular, there is difficulty in separating the idea that the same person is resurrected from the idea that an identical copy – with the potential of many other identical copies – comes to life.

Point 1 claims that the final end for human beings is the timeless Beatific Vision of God, 2 requires a realm of disembodied spirits, and

233

3 implies an everlasting spatio/temporal kingdom. None of these need be required if eternal life is only a different quality of life in this world.

Questions for consideration

a) Do you think you will survive death? If so, in what form will you survive?

b) If you will survive death, how would you know if whatever it is that survives is you rather than a replica of you?

c) If there is a life after death, what might it be like? Would a body be required?

d) If, after the death of your body, your brain was transplanted into a biological robot so that you could operate the robot's body, would you have survived death?

e) If you were cloned, would the clone be you?

f) Can one experience eternal life in this life? If so, what would it mean?

POSTSCRIPT

NINETEEN

And so ...

The challenge facing theology

It all used to be so simple. Some people believed in God and others did not, and the argument was between these two groups. Today, two separate questions arise:

1 What does it mean to say that God exists (this is separate from the different question 'What does it *mean* to believe in or trust in God?' as to trust in God affects the way we live our lives), and
2 What makes the statement 'God exists' true.

Issues of meaning and truth are closely related, but they are different issues. The central issue in the next century facing theologians and many religious believers who want to think about their faith will, in my view, be the issue of what claim is being made when language about God is held to be true. Essentially, as we have seen, realism and anti-realism form two basic positions, although the issue can become much more complicated with a distinction being drawn between Naive, Critical, Internal and Metaphysical realists. However, the basic distinction outlined above still remains.

Just how important is this debate? In some ways the issue does not matter at all. Christian supporters of all the views we have been considering maintain that the central Christian claims are true, even if their understanding of the meaning of these claims differs. Even more important, they all maintain that Christianity calls us to a different way of living, that human beings are called to reject the values of materialism and their own selfish interests in favour of self-giving love for others and the path of virtue. There is a very widespread agreement between supporters of the different views about the alternative lifestyle you and I are called to adopt.

The Danish philosopher and theologian Søren Kierkegaard said: 'As you have lived, so have you believed.' It may well be that our lives and actions are more important than the details of our propositional beliefs. Even Jesus recognised this: he clearly said that it was not those who said, 'Lord, Lord' who truly followed him, but those who showed compassion, who looked after the sick, the imprisoned and others in need. The most intelligent philosopher does not necessarily make the best Christian. There is, indeed, a real danger that preoccupation with the enjoyment of exploring ideas can lead an individual away from the life of love that the Christian path involves.

There is, therefore, a great unity between supporters of the varying views. Having said this, however, there are very significant differences as well, as we have seen during the course of this book. One way to go straight to the heart of the differences between the views we have looked at is to consider what you think happened on Easter Day.

Did Jesus rise from the dead after his crucifixion as an individual with his existing memories? Did Jesus literally survive death? Supporters of the different views we have looked at will answer this question in different ways:

i Those who are realists and who believe in the wholly simple, timeless God will maintain that Jesus did, indeed rise from the dead as an individual. He appeared to his disciples after his death and then ascended to heaven, where he remains what he never ceased to be: the wholly simple, timeless Second Person of the Trinity. Jesus, therefore, after his ascension was no longer an individual in the way he was on earth. As we have seen, the wholly simple, timeless God has no body and is not a person or an individual as we understand the term. Rather, the wholly simple, timeless God took flesh and became a human being and, relinquishing the flesh on his death, is once again what God never ceased to be, the wholly simple, timeless God.

ii Those who are realists and who believe that God is everlasting will claim that Jesus did, indeed, rise from the dead as an individual. He appeared to his disciples after his death and then ascended to heaven where he remains individual and personal, the Second Person of the tri-relational Trinity.

iii Those who affirm the anti-realist approach will say that Jesus lives on after his death in the community of believers. Wherever two or three are gathered together in Jesus' name, there Jesus is with them. They do not, of course, affirm a creator God who is independent of the universe and yet sustains it, but will nevertheless be ready to maintain that God exists within the community of believers who remember him.

Supporters of the first two views believe in a creator God who inter-acts with the universe. A personal relationship between this God and the individual is, therefore, possible. Christianity is at least partly about a personal, two-way 'I/Thou' love-relationship with this God which is lived out in lives of self-giving love for those around us. Advocates of this approach may, although need not necessarily, maintain that the individual survives death and that men and women were created for a fellowship with God which begins on this earth but continues after death as well. Survival of death is, for them, a reality. Generally, although not always, advocates of these two views will maintain that God can act in the world, and this will influence their understanding of prayer, miracles and life after death. These claims are not insignificant, and many believers may feel that without the constant presence of this God, the Christian life is not one that can be easily lived. The anti-realists are likely to disagree and to claim that for believers to continue to maintain that there is a Being of Spirit referred to as the creator God and that a relationship with this God is possible is a relic of thinking from a bygone age. Insistence on this sort of God is now an impediment to belief and is, frankly, incredible – it is a position that can no longer be maintained in a rational and scientific world. The value, meaning and purpose of the Christian life still remains, however.

The issue of reference

The anti-realist position is persuasive and an increasing, even if still small, minority of priests, teachers and others accept it. The attractions are obvious. Proofs for the existence of God are irrelevant and there are no absolute truths, just truths that are accepted within a given form of life into which people are educated or 'initiated'. Within the form of life, questions about doctrine and meaning arise, but these are internal to the religious language game. To the Christian it will be true that God is trinitarian and Jesus rose from the dead, but these will not be true to the Muslim and the two claims do not conflict.

On this view, truth is only to be found within a form of life: there is no neutral standpoint, no place that is not some place (within some form of life) from which the world can be viewed. Truth cannot be looked for independent of context, culture and society. Advocates of this approach will see theology as essentially contextual and concerned with the grammar of belief – with what may or may not be said within a particular faith community. This depends on the particular period of history and the society in which theological language is used. There are no absolute truths. More traditional believers, however, may want to reject this view and may want to hold that 'God exists' is true if and only if this refers to the God who created and sustains the universe and is independent of it, in other words, they maintain a realist position about truth. In this case they are faced with an immediate problem: *How, in the face of conflicting belief systems, do they justify their claim that language corresponds or successfully refers?*

The traditional Christian may want to insist that Christianity is true *if and only if* Jesus rose from the dead as an individual. It is not just the case that his followers told themselves stories to this effect (see *The Puzzle of the Gospels*, P. Vardy and M. Mill, HarperCollins, 1995, Ch. 1). The issue of truth and falsity, it may be claimed, depends on an historical claim. To be sure, this claim may not be *provable*, but it is only the anti-realist who will maintain that

1 The truth of a statement, and 2. The verification of a statement

are necessarily linked. The realist claims that 1 and 2 are separate issues. Just as in science 'the ways things are' may be independent of our language games and we may try to reach out to capture and discover reality, so religion may also be attempting a similar exercise. Some religious claims may be true and others false and this may be because they either succeed or fail in successfully depicting ultimate reality.

However, if traditional believers are to maintain that 'God exists' is true because it successfully refers to the God who exists independently of the universe God has created and sustained, how do they show that this is the case? And do they *have* to show this at all? These are central issues today for anyone who wants to maintain a realist understanding of God. Natural Theology (represented by the arguments for the existence of God) apparently does not succeed in establishing reference as so many of the assumptions on which the arguments are based can be challenged. Reformed Epistemology seeks to appeal to faith and to revelation to establish reference but, in the absence of rational criteria, finds difficulty in convincing anyone who does not share the belief in question. Also, given multiple claims to truth by many different creeds and religions, it seems particularly vulnerable to the anti-realist challenge. However, as we have seen (pp. 138ff.) the anti-realist position is itself vulnerable: it is prescriptive and does not do what it claims to do, which is to reflect what believers themselves say about religious faith.

This book has left you with no answers, but only, perhaps, with more questions than you had at the outset. This is the nature of the faith journey, a journey that continually seeks truth amid great uncertainty. In spite of all the advances made by science, in spite of all the insights of philosophy, the questions about God remain to challenge us and continue to be among the most important questions that each of us has to answer. They will not go away, nor leave us alone. Great literature, art and music all affirm the importance of the search and, in the end, perhaps, we have to stake our lives on claims to truth about which we may always have to admit some element of doubt. Socrates said that he could not prove the immortality of the soul but was ready to stake his life on the 'if' that the soul exists. Perhaps we need to ask ourselves about how we will stake our lives. Many believers will maintain, with Luther, that after all their philosophy they can only say, 'Here I stand, I can do no other,' and perhaps this stand in itself is a greater pointer to the reality of God than any philosophy.

One final point needs to be made. This has been a book about philosophy of religion: it has used reason to try to understand a little about the claims made by religious believers and the different ways in which these can be understood. However, it is at least possible that philosophy may 'do violence' to religious belief by interpreting it in terms that undermine its reality. It may be that faith goes beyond reason and that some of the most important things in life such as love, beauty and religious faith cannot be reduced to rational analysis. Too great a concentration, therefore, on philosophy alone may fail to reveal other aspects of reality that are of great importance. Art, literature, music or even walking alone in the open fields or under the night sky may give us perspectives on life that philosophers fail to see. In our rush to understand, we may lose sight of the fact that we first have to be still and silent before we understand anything. Pooh Bear was a bear of very little brain who did not consider himself wise and would have been at a loss to understand this book, but perhaps Pooh had a wisdom that went beyond words. He stood by his friends, he was gentle and compassionate and he is my favourite bear precisely because these things matter more than all the words in the world.

Questions for consideration

a) What do you think happened on Easter Day? Did Jesus rise from the dead as an individual?

b) Which view of God do you consider to be most plausible?

c) Do you consider that religious people should only believe what they can understand, or what can be rationally justified?

d) If you fall in love, will you be able to give rational reasons to explain this?

e) Why might silence be important?

f) Who was wiser, Pooh Bear, Rabbit or Owl?

Suggested Further Reading

Peter Vardy, *What is Truth?* (University of New South Wales, 1999)

Arguments for the existence of God

Richard Swinburne, *The Existence of God* (Oxford University Press, 1979)

J. L. Mackie, *The Miracle of Theism* (Oxford University Press, 1982)

J. C. A. Gaskin, *The Quest for Eternity* (Penguin, 1984)

David Hume, *Dialogues Concerning Natural Religion* (Hackett, 1980)

J. S. Mill, *Three Essays on Religion* (P. Thoemmes, 1993)

John Hick, *The Existence of God* (Macmillan, 1974)

Michael Peterson and others, *Reason and Religious Belief* (Oxford University Press, 1998)

Religious experience

Nicholas Lash, *Easter in Ordinary* (University of Notre Dame Press, 1990)

William James, *Varieties of Religious Experience* (Penguin, 1982)

Caroline Franks Davies, *The Evidential Force of Religious Experience* (Oxford University Press, 1989)

Introduction to Aquinas and the Thomist approach

F. Copleston SJ, *Aquinas* (Search Press, 1976). Probably the best introduction.

Brian Davies OP, *Thinking about God* (Chapman, 1985)

G. J. Hughes, *The Nature of God* (Routledge, 1995). Excellent but difficult.

Anthony Kenny, *Aquinas: A Selection of Critical Essays* (Doubleday, 1969)

Janet Martin Soskice, *Metaphor and Religious Language* (Clarendon Press, 1985)

The anti-realist revisionary view of religious language

Ludwig Wittgenstein, *On Certainty* (Harper Torch Books, 1969)

R. Trigg, *Reality at Risk*: a Defence of Realism (Harvester, 1989)

B. Clack and B. Clack, *The Philosophy of Religion* (Polity, 1998)

D. Z. Phillips, *Faith after Foundationalism* (Routledge, 1988)

Gareth Moore OP, *Believing in God, a Philosophic Essay* (T. & T. Clarke, 1989)

Don Cupitt, *The Long-Legged Fly* (SCM Press, 1987)

— *Taking Leave for God* (SCM Press, 1980)

Scott Cowdell, *Atheist Priest* (SCM Press, 1988)

Dan R. Stivel, *The Philosophy of Religious Language* (Blackwell, 1996)

Prayer

D. Z. Phillips, *The Concept of Prayer* (Blackwell, 1981)

V. Brummer, *What Are We Doing When We Pray?* (SPCK, 1984)

C. S. Lewis, *Letters to Malcolm* (Fount, 1966)

Miracles and God's action in the world

M. Wiles, *God's Action in the World* (SCM Press, 1986)

Richard Swinburne, *The Concept of Miracle* (Macmillan, 1970)

N. Pike, *God and Timelessness* (Schocken, 1979)

T. V. Morris, *The Concept of God* (section by Stump & Kretzmann, Oxford University Press, 1987)

Eternal life

D. Z. Phillips, *Death and Immortality* (Macmillan, 1970)

John Hick, *Death and Eternal Life* (Collins, 1976)

Gilbert Ryle, *The Concept of Mind* (Penguin, 1970). Classic argument against the dualist position.

Karl Rahner, *The Theology of Death* (Nelson, 1961)
John Donnelly, *Language, Metaphysics and Death* (Fordham
  University Press, 1978. Series of articles covering related topics).

Omnipotence and omniscience

T. V. Morris, *The Concept of God*. Chapters with these headings
  (Oxford University Press, 1987)
Boethius, *The Consolation of Philosophy*, trans. V. Watts (Penguin,
  1969)
R. H. Nash, *The Concept of God* (Zondervan, 1983)
G. J. Hughes, *The Nature of God* (Routledge, 1995)

General

P. Quinn and C. Taliaferno, *A Companion to Philosophy of Religion*
  (Blackwell, 1977). An excellent compilation of articles.